Contents

LAW LIBRARY OF CONGRESS

BOTSWANA

WILDLIFE TRAFFICKING AND POACHING

Executive Summary

Botswana has a robust regulatory regime governing the conservation and management of its wildlife. This regime bans poaching as well as trade in animals, trophies, meat, and articles made out of trophies without the proper permits or in violation of the terms of a license or permit. Violation of any of the applicable laws entails various forms of penalties including fines, prison terms, forfeiture of tools used in the commission of a crime as well as the fruits of the crime, and revocation of licenses. Offenses involving certain vulnerable animals and recidivism result in greater penalties.

Although the principal enforcer of the regulatory regime is the Department of Wildlife and National Parks (DWNP), the Botswana Police Service (BPS) and the Botswana Defense Force (BDF) also share enforcement responsibilities. The DWNP and the BPS enjoy wide search and seizure powers and focus on local enforcement, while the BDF's role is by and large directed at cross-border crime syndicates, intelligence gathering, and working in coordination with institutions of neighboring states, including conducting joint sting operations.

I. Introduction

The importance of wildlife protection in Botswana cannot be overstated. The success of the tourism industry in the country rests heavily on its wildlife.[1] The country's wildlife estate makes up more than one-third of its landmass, with its national parks and game reserves comprising 17% of the estate and its wildlife management area encompassing over 20%.[2] Okavango Delta, which is the largest inland wetland habitat in the world, is said to be the biggest draw for tourists that visit the country.[3] About 90% of all visitors of the country come for "a

---

[1] Dan Henk, *The Botswana Defence Force and the War Against Poachers in Southern Africa*, 16(2) SMALL WARS & INSURGENCIES 170, 172 (June 2005), *available at* http://www.rhinoresourcecenter.com/pdf_files/124/1243173877.pdf.

[2] *About Us*, DEPARTMENT OF WILDLIFE AND NATIONAL PARKS, http://www.mewt.gov.bw/DWNP/article.php?id_mnu=41 (last visited Dec. 20, 2012).

[3] The European Union, Botswana Tourism Development Programme – Tourism Master Plan 4 (May 2000), *available at* the Botswana Tourism website, http://www.botswanatourism.co.bw/assests/tourism_master_plan.pdf.

wildlife and wilderness-based vacation" and revenue from tourism accounts for 12% of the country's gross domestic product.[4]

Various policy documents and laws affect wildlife issues in Botswana. Among these are the Tribal Grazing Lands Policy of 1975; the Wildlife Conservation Policy of 1986,[5] which is currently under review; the Tourism Policy of 1990; the National Conservation Strategy of 1990; and the Tourism Act of 1992.[6] However, the principal legislation governing wildlife resources and their habitat, including hunting issues, is the Wildlife Conservation and National Parks Act of 1992 (WCNPA)[7] and its subsidiary legislation.[8] Among other things, this legislation implements the Convention on International Trade in Endangered Species of Wild Fauna and Flora (CITES)[9] and incorporates the text of the Convention including "any Appendices and any Resolutions of the Conference of the Parties."[10]

Although allowed in limited instances, hunting in Botswana is heavily regulated. The country allows hunting, including commercial hunting, in what are known as controlled areas and on private land.[11] It also allows hunting of "partially protected animals."[12] Hunting protected game animals[13] is limited to specific purposes including disease control, public safety, or other public functions such as education, scientific research, or obtaining a specimen for a

---

[4] *Id.* at 5; *Botswana to Ban Wildlife Hunting*, HOWZITMSN (Nov. 29, 2012), http://news.howzit.msn.com/ botswana-to-ban-wildlife-hunting.

[5] Wildlife Conservation Policy, Government Paper No. 1 of 1986 (Government Printer, July 10, 1986), *available at* the Botswana Environmental Information System, UNDP website, http://www1.eis.gov. bw/EIS/Policies/ Environmental%20Policies/Wildlife%20Conservation%20Policy.pdf.

[6] DEPARTMENT OF WILDLIFE AND NATIONAL PARKS, *supra* note 2.

[7] Wildlife Conservation and National Parks Act of 1992, VI LAWS OF BOTSWANA, Cap. 38:0 (rev. ed. 2011), *available at* the Botswana e-Laws website, http://www .elaws.gov.bw/wondersbtree.php?m= PRINCIPAL&v=VI&vp=&t=WILDLIFE%20CONSERVATION%20AND%20NATIONAL%20PARKS&st=&pt= 38:01#940.

[8] Wildlife Conservation and National Parks: Subsidiary Legislation, VI LAWS OF BOTSWANA, Cap. 38:0 (rev. ed. 2011), http://www.elaws.gov.bw/wondersbtree.php?m=SUBSIDIARY&v=VI&vp=&t=WILDLIFE %20CONSERVATION%20AND%20NATIONAL%20PARKS:%20SUBSIDIARY%20LEGISLATION%20previo usly%20ampquotFAUNA%20CONSERVATIONampquot&st=FAUNA%20CONSERVATION%20MANNYELA NONG%20GAME%20RESERVE%20REGULATIONS&pt=38:01#1801.

[9] Convention on International Trade in Endangered Species of Wild Fauna and Flora, Mar. 3, 1973, 993 U.N.T.S. 243, http://www.cites.org/eng/disc/text.php.

[10] Wildlife Conservation and National Parks Act § 2.

[11] *Id.* §§ 16 & 20.

[12] *Id.* § 18. These are leopard, lion, elephant, chobe bushbuck, sable antelope, and eland. *Id.*, sched. 7, pt. I.

[13] These are "night-ape, pangolin, aardwolf, brown hyaena, cheetah, serval, blackfooted cat, wild dog, otter, honey badger, civet, antbear, rock dassie, yellow-spotted dassie, rhinoceros, hippopotamus, giraffe, klipspringer, oribi, sharpe's steenbok, mountain reedbuck, waterbuck, puku, roan antelope, vaal rhebok, all pelicans, all herons, all egrets, all bitterns, hammerkop, all storks, all ibises, spoonbill, all flamingoes, secretary bird, all vultures, all falcons, all kites, all eagles, all buzzards, all parrowhawks, all goshawks, all harriers, all cranes, kori bustard, stanley, bustard, all jacanas, fishing owl, narina trogon, python." *Id.*, sched. 6.

museum.[14] However, most hunting requires a permit or license. In addition, there are various prohibitions including on hunting protected game animals, hunting in prohibited areas, hunting or capturing game animals at night or by using blinding lights, hunting during the closed season, and hunting using certain prohibited methods.[15]

News sources indicate that Botswana will impose further limits on hunting in the near future. Citing concerns about declining wildlife species, authorities recently announced that they will ban commercial hunting from January 2014.[16] According to a statement released by the government, commercial hunting of wildlife in "public or controlled hunting areas" will be indefinitely suspended.[17] This will affect currently active hunting concessions including in northern Okavango Delta and the parks in the Kalahari region.[18]

The WCNPA also heavily regulates trade in animals, trophies, meat, and articles made out of trophies. It does this by imposing licensing and permit requirements for dealing in, importing/exporting, or transporting through Botswana any animal, trophy, meat, or eggs.[19]

Violations of the provisions of the WCNPA are heavily penalized. Penalties involve a combination of fines and prison terms. In addition, the fruits of a crime as well as the items used in its commission may be subject to forfeiture.[20] Significantly, the WCNPA imposes evidentiary and procedural burdens on persons suspected of violating its provisions that are not typically part of criminal legal regimes. One example in this regard is the legal presumption that a person who enters private land with a weapon is there to hunt illegally unless he can prove otherwise or prove that he had the owner's permission.[21]

II. Poaching and Trafficking in Wildlife

A. Hunting in Certain Places

While it is legal to hunt in places designated as controlled hunting areas, doing so without a license is an offense.[22] There are few exceptions. Botswana citizens who principally depend on hunting for food and who have been issued special waivers to hunt animals other than game

---

[14] *Id.* § 17.

[15] *Id.* §§ 17, 45, 55 & 57.

[16] *Botswana to Ban Hunting Over Wildlife Species Decline*, BBC (Nov. 29, 2012), http://www.bbc.co.uk/news/world-africa-20544251.

[17] *Botswana to Ban Wildlife Hunting*, AFP (Nov. 20, 2012), http://www.google.com/hostednews/afp/article/ALeqM5ibc9qgE261AAxhFF37Ye-updXFGg?docId=CNG.9aaaa56d53d58d95e0d67d4eec36888a.111.

[18] *Botswana to Ban Wildlife Hunting*, RADIO NEW ZEALAND NEWS (Nov. 30, 2012), http://www.radionz.co.nz/news/world/122236/botswana-to-ban-wildlife-hunting.

[19] Wildlife Conservation and National Parks Act §§ 62–66.

[20] *Id.* §§ 71 & 75.

[21] *Id.* § 49.

[22] *Id.* § 16.

animals do not need a license.[23]   Similarly, those who have been granted permits to kill or capture any animal for certain specific purposes such as education or scientific research may hunt in controlled areas without a license.[24]   Finally, those who have been granted a permit to kill animals other than protected game animals for the purpose of disease control, public safety, or property protection do not need a license to hunt in controlled areas.[25]   Hunting any animal in a controlled area without a license or in violation of the terms of a license is punishable by 2,000 Botswana Pula (P) (about US$256) and two years' imprisonment in addition to any other applicable penalties.[26]

Similarly, hunting is allowed on private land under the concept of "landholder's privileges," which applies to landowners, lessees, and the employees or relations of such landowners/lessees, all of whom must be citizens or residents of Botswana.[27]   Private land may also be utilized for commercial hunting, known as the use of landholder's privileges for profit.[28] While hunting of protected and partially protected animals by those with landholder's privileges may be undertaken without a license, those authorized to use landholder's privileges for profit must hold a license or permit, and it is the landholder's responsibility to ensure that authorized hunters are in possession of the requisite licenses or permits.[29]   In both cases, a landholder is required to keep records of the hunters and all animals killed.[30]   In addition, in both cases, the law imposes a limit as to how many game animals may be killed each year on private land. For instance, a maximum of ten zebras a year may be killed on private land; a violation of this requirement is an offense punishable by P500 (about US$64) and a six-month prison term unless a penalty is already provided under a different provision.[31]

B. Hunting of Certain Animals

In addition to geographic limitations on hunting, the WCNPA imposes a ban on the hunting of certain of animals. Hunting of any animal in Botswana requires a license or a permit with two exceptions: anyone may hunt a non-designated invertebrate animal without a license outside of a national park or a game reserve, and any Botswana citizen may hunt without a license any non-designated animal for consumption.[32]

Hunting of partially protected game animals, designated game animals, or game birds without a license is an offense for which the WCNPA imposes different penalties depending on

---

[23] *Id.* § 30.

[24] *Id.* § 39.

[25] *Id.* § 49.

[26] *Id.* § 16.

[27] *Id.* § 20.

[28] *Id.* §21.

[29] *Id.* §§ 20 & 21.

[30] *Id.* § 22.

[31] *Id.* § 20 & sched. 8.

[32] *Id.* § 19.

the gravity of the offense. Hunting any game animal partially protected throughout Botswana (leopard, lion, elephant, chobe bushbuck, sable antelope, and eland) without a license is an offense punishable by a fine of P5,000 (about US$638) and five years' imprisonment.[33] If the animal in question is an elephant, a dramatically higher penalty of P50,000 (about US$ 6,375) in fines and a ten-year prison term are applicable.[34] Hunting of a designated game animal (including baboon, caracal, wildcat, and zebra) without a license is also an offense punishable by a fine of P2,000 (about US$255) and two years in prison.[35] In addition, hunting a designated game bird (such as spur-wing goose, Egyptian goose, whitefaced duck, and snipe) without a license is an offense punishable by P1,000 (about US$128) in fines and a one-year prison term.[36] If the offense involves non-designated animals or a violation of the terms of a license, the penalties are relatively mild—a fine of P500 and six months' imprisonment.[37]

Hunting of protected game animals (including cheetah, wild dog, otter, rhinoceros, all pelicans, and all flamingos) is prohibited.[38] There are a few exceptions to this rule: such hunting may be permitted if it is for certain particular uses such as education and scientific research, or for the purpose of disease control, public safety, or protection of property.[39] Two classes of penalties are applicable for violations of this ban. The general penalty imposed for an offense under this provision is a fine of P10,000 (about US$1,275) and seven years' imprisonment.[40] If the offense involves a rhinoceros the applicable penalties are dramatically higher—a fine of P100,000 (about US$12,750) and fifteen years' imprisonment.[41]

There are further exceptions applicable to bans on hunting of any animal, including instances in which hunting is permitted to protect property, for self-defense, or for the defense of others. An owner or occupier of land or his agent may "kill any animal which caused, is causing or threatens to cause damage to any livestock, crops, water installation or fence of such land."[42] However, this does not apply to cheetahs[43] or lions (although in certain specific instances killing a lion may be allowed),[44] or to animals in a national park or game reserve,[45] and the exception

---

[33] *Id.* §§ 18 & 19.

[34] *Id.* § 19.

[35] *Id.*

[36] *Id.*

[37] *Id.*

[38] *Id.* § 17.

[39] *Id.*

[40] *Id.*

[41] *Id.*

[42] *Id.* § 46.

[43] Wildlife Conservation and National Parks Act, Wildlife Conservation and National Parks (Cheetahs) (Killing Suspension) Order, S.I. 26, § 2 (Apr. 22, 2005).

[44] Wildlife Conservation and National Parks Act, Wildlife Conservation and National Parks (Lions) (Killing Suspension) Order, S.I. 26, § 2 (Apr. 22, 2005).

[45] Wildlife Conservation and National Parks Act § 46.

does not authorize the use of "any poisoned weapon, pitfall or snare for the killing of any animal."[46]   The law authorizes killing or wounding any animal in self-defense or in defense of others if it is "immediately and absolutely necessary."[47]   If a person who does not have a license kills a game animal in self-defense or in defense of others, the person is required to report the killing and deliver the trophy to a wildlife officer or police station. Failure to do so is an offense punishable by a fine of P500 and six months' imprisonment.[48]

C. Hunting Methods

The WCNPA prohibits various hunting methods that give hunters undue advantage over their prey. Unless otherwise authorized, it prohibits hunting at night,[49] the use of blinding lights to hunt, and hunting during closed seasons.[50] A violation of any of these bans is an offense punishable by a fine of P5,000 and a five-year prison term in addition to penalties that may be imposed for violations of other provisions of the law.[51]   Other generally prohibited methods include

- shooting at a game animal from any vehicle, aircraft, or mechanically propelled vessel;

- getting closer than 200 meters to any animal for the purpose of hunting the animal;

- surrounding an animal with fire or causing any grass or bush fire for the purpose of hunting; or

- use of a weapon other than a hunting rifle, a shot gun, or a dog.[52]

There are certain exceptions to some of these bans, the most typical being the use of a prohibited method when the hunting involves an animal causing damage to property or is in self-defense. A violation of any of the above bans is an offense punishable by a fine of P5,000 and five years' imprisonment.[53]

---

[46] *Id.*

[47] *Id.* § 47.

[48] *Id.*

[49] "In any year from the 1st March to 30th September means the period of time between half past six in the evening and six o'clock in the morning, and from the 1st October to the last day of February means the period of time between half past seven in the evening and half past five o'clock in the morning." *Id.* § 2.

[50] *Id.* §§ 55 & 56. There are of course exceptions to these bans, including instances in which a person has a permit specifically allowing hunting at night, the use of blinding light, or hunting during a closed season as well as hunting to protect damage to property or hunting in self-defense. *Id.*

[51] *Id.*

[52] *Id.* § 57.

[53] *Id.*

D. Attempt and Other Offenses

A person does not have to engage in illegal hunting in order to commit an offense under the WCNPA; certain acts that indicate that a person plans to engage in poaching are also banned. For instance, a person who enters private land without the permission of the owner for the purpose of hunting commits an offense punishable by a fine of P1,000 (about US$128) and one year in prison.[54] In this case, the controlling law shifts the burden of proof to the accused by making a presumption that a person found on any land in possession of a weapon is deemed to be in violation of the law unless he can prove otherwise or prove that he had the owner's consent.[55] Similarly, in certain circumstances the law makes conveyance of a loaded weapon other than a pistol, including while traveling along a road to which there is public access, an offense punishable by a fine of P1,000 and a one-year prison term.[56]

E. Sale, Export, and Import Restrictions

The WCNPA bans the import to, export from, transport through, or re-export from Botswana of any "animal, or trophy, meat or eggs" without a permit.[57] A violation of this provision is an offense and entails a penalty of P10,000 in fines and a seven-year prison term.[58] The law also prohibits selling or otherwise dealing in, or manufacturing any articles from, any trophy illegally obtained in or imported into Botswana.[59] A violation of this provision is an offense punishable by a fine of P5,000 and five years' imprisonment.[60]

When an elephant or rhinoceros is involved, the applicable penalty is significantly higher. If the commission of an offense involves an elephant or its trophy the penalty is a fine of P50,000 and ten years' imprisonment.[61] If the offense involves a rhinoceros the penalty is P100,000 in fines and a ten-year prison term.[62]

The WCNPA also makes selling "any game animal or "non-designated animal,"[63] or "meat, eggs or trophy of any animal" without a proper permit an offense punishable by P1,000 in fines and a one-year prison term.[64] It establishes a presumption that any animal or animal

---

[54] *Id.* § 49.

[55] *Id.*

[56] *Id.* § 50.

[57] *Id.* § 62.

[58] *Id.*

[59] *Id.* § 64.

[60] *Id.*

[61] *Id.*

[62] *Id.*

[63] A "non-designated animal" is defined as "any animal which is not a game animal." *Id.* § 2.

[64] *Id.* § 60.

product found in any business establishment and for which there is no permit is intended for an illegal sale.[65]

III. Penalties of General Application

The above sections discussing wildlife protection offenses also outline the penalties associated with each offense. In addition to these penalties, the controlling law imposes forfeiture penalties applicable to all such offenses, including forfeiture of the fruits of an offense and the tools used to commit it. Therefore, any animal killed in violation of any provision of the controlling law and any trophy or part of such animal is automatically forfeited to the government.[66] Similarly, if any violation of a provision of the law involves a trophy, the trophy is forfeited to the government.[67]

In certain instances the tools used in the commission of an offense are also subject to forfeiture. Whenever a person is convicted of an offense punishable by a fine of P2,000 or more, the court is required by law to order the forfeiture to the government of any tools used in the commission of the offense, including a weapon, trap, or vehicle.[68] In all other lesser offenses, the court has the discretion to order forfeiture of such tools.[69]

In addition to fines, prison terms, and forfeiture, all offenses punishable by a fine of at least P1,000 automatically trigger the revocation of the offender's license, permit, authority, or permission issued under the WCNPA unless the court says otherwise.[70]

Finally, recidivism in relation to any offense under the WNCPA triggers significantly higher sentences. A second or subsequent conviction under any of the provisions of the controlling law automatically triggers a higher penalty in which "the maximum penalty prescribed for such offense shall be increased by fifty percent."[71]

IV. Enforcement Authority

The Department of Wildlife and National Parks (DWNP), one of several departments at the Ministry of Environment, Wildlife and Tourism, enjoys wide-ranging powers to enforce the WCNPA through its wildlife officers, including the Director of the Department, any other public officer of the Department charged with the implementation and administration of the provisions of the controlling law, and honorary officers to the extent of their authorization to act on behalf of the Department.[72] While the DWNP is the principal enforcer of the WCNPA, it is not the

---

[65] *Id.*

[66] *Id.* § 71.

[67] *Id.*

[68] *Id.* § 75.

[69] *Id.*

[70] *Id.*

[71] *Id.* § 79.

[72] *Id.* §§ 2 & 3; *see also* DEPARTMENT OF WILDLIFE AND NATIONAL PARKS, *supra* note 2.

only enforcer. The Botswana Police Service also has some enforcement powers.[73] In addition, the Botswana Defense Force (BDF) has since 1987 played an increasingly prominent role in antipoaching operations in support of the DWNP and the police.[74]

Wildlife and police officers have broad enforcement powers and are authorized to conduct warrantless searches and seizures if they have reasonable grounds to believe that a person has violated the WCNPA.[75] For instance, a wildlife or police officer may "stop, seize and search any vehicle, boat or aircraft which he believes to have been used in the commission of the offence, or to contain anything which might provide evidence of the offence."[76] He may also seize anything—including an animal, meat, trophy, or weapon—reasonably believed to be evidence of an offense.[77]

A wildlife officer also has limited prosecutorial power and may charge and summon for court appearance a person suspected of committing an offense under the WCNPA punishable by a fine of up to P500 and up to six months in prison.[78]

In addition, the BDF plays a major role in enforcing the WCNPA. Although no statutory authority for its role was located, one scholarly source indicates that the BDF's involvement in antipoaching activities began in 1987 in large part to support the DWNP, whose antipoaching arm at the time was unable to effectively carry out its mission.[79] Although at the beginning the BDF's Commando Squadron was the only unit involved in antipoaching activities, by 1989 the mission was broadened to include all units of the BDF.[80] The BDF's antipoaching operations are aimed more at cross-border poaching by armed gangs than at local meat poachers.[81] The BDF works closely with DWNP and the police in planning and executing its operations.[82] It also works with countries in the region through a Joint Military Commission in which members share intelligence and participate in joint sting operations.[83]

Prepared by Hanibal Goitom
Foreign Law Specialist
January 2013

---

[73] *Id.* § 73.

[74] Henk, *supra* note 1, at 177–81; Vince Crawley, *Botswana Troops Get Up Close and Personal with Wildlife Before Anti-Poaching Missions*, AFRICOM (Nov. 9, 2011), http://www.africom.mil/getArticle.asp?art=7422.

[75] Wildlife Conservation and National Parks Act § 73.

[76] *Id.*

[77] *Id.*

[78] *Id.* § 76.

[79] Henk, *supra* note 1, at 176.

[80] *Id.* at 178.

[81] *Id.* at. 183.

[82] *Id* at 185.

[83] *Id.*

2013–008667

LAW LIBRARY OF CONGRESS

CENTRAL AFRICAN REPUBLIC

WILDLIFE TRAFFICKING AND POACHING

Executive Summary

The Central African Republic (CAR) possesses an extensive and well-developed legislative framework for the protection of wildlife, particularly pertaining to elephants and ivory products. Hunting activities are permitted under certain circumstances in certain areas of the country with prior authorization from the central government. Penalties range from fines to imprisonment, and enforcement is entrusted to a number of different government agencies.

I. General Legal Framework Concerning Wildlife Protection in the CAR

A. Background

The CAR's legislation concerning wildlife protection is particularly diverse and fragmented, as it consists of varied legal instruments that either overlap or regulate the same matter. In consequence, it is almost impossible to determine with absolute certainty which legal instrument would apply in a specific situation.

The main legislation aimed at protecting wildlife and curbing poaching and illegal trafficking in the CAR is as follows: the Forestry Code of 2008;[1] the Code of the Environment of 2007;[2] Ordinance 85.005 of 1985, Concerning the Elimination of Elephant Hunting;[3] Ordinance 84.062 of 1984, Establishing the Conditions for the Capture and Exportation of Live Wild Animals;[4] Ordinance 84.045 of 1984, Concerning the Protection of Wildlife and the Regulation of Hunting in the Central African Republic;[5] Decree 84.341 of 1984, Establishing the Conditions

---

[1] Code Forestier [Forestry Code] of October 17, 2008, *available at* FAOLEX, the legislative database of the United Nations Food and Agriculture Organization (FAO) legal office, http://faolex.fao.org/docs/pdf/caf107432.pdf.

[2] Law 68 of December 28, 2007, portant Code de l'Environnement en République Centrafricaine [Code of the Environment of the Central African Republic], *available at* http://faolex.fao.org/docs/pdf/caf105925.pdf.

[3] Ordonnance n° 85.005 of January 30, 1985, portant fermeture de la chasse à l'éléphant [Concerning the Elimination of Elephant Hunting], *available at* http://faolex.fao.org/docs/pdf/caf39393.pdf.

[4] Ordonnance n° 84.062 of October 9, 1984 fixant les conditions de capture et d'exportation d'animaux sauvages vivants [Establishing the Conditions for the Capture and Exportation of Live Wild Animals], *available at* http://faolex.fao.org/docs/pdf/caf39394.pdf.

[5] Ordonnance n° 84.045 of July 27, 1984 portant Protection de la Faune Sauvage et Réglementant l'exercice de la Chasse en République Centrafricaine [Concerning the Protection of Wildlife and the Regulation of Hunting in the Central African Republic], *available at* http://faolex.fao.org/cgi-bin/faolex.exe?rec_id=002601&database=faolex&search_type=link&table=result&lang=eng&format_name=@ERALL.

for Obtaining and the Rates for Issuing Permits to Capture Live Wild Animals;[6] Ordinance 81-013 of 1981, Implementing Ordinance n° 80-30, Concerning the Prohibition of the Commercialization of Hunting Products (Ivory);[7] Decree 0633 of 1972, Concerning the Creation of a Professional Identity Card for Hunting Guides Working in the Central African Republic;[8] Law 422/63 of 1963, Amending Law n° 62-343 of 1962, Establishing a Supreme Council for Hunting;[9] Law 62/350 of 1963, Concerning the Organization for the Protection of Plants in the Central African Republic;[10] Decree 62-239 of 1962, Against Poaching During Periods of Livestock Migration;[11] Law 61/276 of 1961, Concerning the Regulation of the Introduction of Hunting Weapons and Munitions by Nonresident Hunters;[12] Law 61/281 of 1961, Regulating the Practice of Hunting and Commercial Hunting Products;[13] and Law 60-126 of 1960, Against the Poaching of Migrant Livestock.[14]

A major government agency with the responsibility for regulating hunting, protecting nature, organizing management and exploitation services for wildlife, creating protected areas, and regulating wildlife tourism is the Supreme Council for Hunting,[15] which is administered by the Ministry of Hunting[16] and the Directorate of Waters, Forests and Hunting.[17]

---

[6] Decree n° 84.341 of October 9, 1984 fixant les conditions d'obtention et les tarifs des permis de capture d'animaux sauvages vivants [Establishing the Conditions for Obtaining and the rates for Issuing of Permits to Capture Live Wild Animals], *available at* http://faolex fao. org/docs/pdf/caf39395.pdf.

[7] Ordonnance n° 81-013 of November 23, 1981 rapportant les dispositions de l'ordonnance n° 80-30 portant interdiction de la commercialisation des produits de la chasse (ivoire) [Implementing the Provisions of Ordinance n° 80-30, Concerning the Prohibition of the Commercialization of Hunting Products (Ivory)], *available at* http://faolex. fao.org/docs/pdf/caf39396.pdf.

[8] Arrêté n° 0633 of October 13, 1972 portant création d'une carte d'identité professionnelle pour les guides de chasse exerçant en République centrafricaine [Concerning the Creation of a Professional Identity Card for Hunting Guides Working in the Central African Republic], *available at* http://faolex.fao.org/docs/pdf/caf4162.pdf.

[9] Loi n° 422/63 of November 15, 1963, modifiant la Loi n° 62-343 du 1962 instituant un Conseil Supérieur de la Chasse [Amending Law n° 62-343 of 1962, Establishing a Supreme Council for Hunting], *available at* http:// faolex.fao.org/docs/pdf/caf39426.pdf.

[10] Loi n° 62/350 of January 4, 1963 relative à l'organisation de la protection des végétaux en République centrafricaine [Concerning the Organization for the Protection of Plants in the Central African Republic], *available at* http://faolex fao.org/docs/pdf/caf7180.pdf.

[11] Décret n° 62-239 of November 5, 1962 contre le braconage en période de transhumance [Against Poaching During Periods of Livestock Migration], *available at* http://faolex fao.org/docs/pdf/caf44471.pdf.

[12] Loi n° 61/276 of December 22, 1961 portant règlementation applicable aux chasseurs non résidents en matière d'introduction d'armes de chasse et de munitions [Concerning the Regulation of the Introduction of Hunting Weapons and Munitions by Nonresident Hunters], *available at* http://faolex fao.org/docs/pdf/caf44469.pdf.

[13] Loi n° 61/281 of December 22, 1961 règlementant l'exercice de la chasse et les produits de la chasse à caractère commercial [Regulating the Practice of Hunting and Commercial Hunting Products], *available at* http:// faolex.fao.org/docs/pdf/caf44470.pdf.

[14] Loi n° 60-126 of June 20, 1960 contre le braconage des transhumants [Against the Poaching of Migrant Livestock], *available at* http://faolex fao. org/docs/pdf/caf44464.pdf.

[15] Law 422/63 of 1963, art. 2.

[16] *Id*. art. 10.

[17] *Id*. art. 13.

B. Restricted Areas and Periods

Hunting is forbidden in integral natural reserves,[18] national parks, wildlife and hunting reserves, urban areas, and in other areas.[19]

Private persons may be authorized to access hunting areas for the purposes of hunting, tourism, or observation under terms established in a contract signed with the ministry in charge of wildlife.[20] This ministry may establish open and closed hunting seasons throughout the year and throughout the national territory.[21]

C. Classification of Wildlife for Regulatory Purposes

Wildlife is classified as (a) fully protected, (b) partially protected, and (c) ordinary game.[22]

Fully protected animals are those included in List A of Annex 2 to Ordinance 84.045 of 1984, and are subject to the following restrictions: (a) their capture, as well as the collection or destruction of their eggs, larvae, nests, or lodgings is absolutely forbidden;[23] and (b) their exportation by private individuals is strictly forbidden, with the exception of holders of commercial capture permits.[24]

Partially protected animals are those included in List B of Annex 2 to Ordinance 84.045 of 1984, and their hunting is permitted in accordance with the applicable legislation.[25]

The possession or transportation of fully or partially protected animals listed in Articles 18 and 19 of Law 60/140 on the Protection of Nature list fully or partially protected animals the possession or transportation of which is absolutely forbidden without prior authorization, with the exception of commercial capture permits mentioned in article 2 of Law 61/281 of 1961.[26] This list includes leopards, cheetahs, hyenas, gorillas, chimpanzees, rhinoceros, hippopotamus, giraffes, and crocodiles, for example, as fully protected animals; and lions, elephants, warthogs, mongooses, and pythons, among others, as partially protected animals. The complete list of fully

---

[18] Integral natural reserves are "areas devoid of all human presence." Ordinance 84.045 of 1984, art. 2. Also according to article 2 of Ordinance 84.045 of 1984, entry into these areas or overflying them at altitudes of less than 200 meters is forbidden, except by prior authorization obtained in accordance with articles 101 and 102 of Ordinance 84.045 of 1984. *Id.*

[19] *Id.* art. 66.

[20] *Id.* arts. 68–71.

[21] *Id.* art. 64.

[22] *Id.* art. 27.

[23] *Id.* art. 28.

[24] Law 61/281 of 1961, art. 16.

[25] Ordinance 84.045 of 1984, art. 30.

[26] Law 61/281 of 1961, art. 13.

protected animals can be found in documents referred to in footnotes 23 and 41 of this report, and partially protected animals are listed in documents referred to in footnotes 23 and 41.

Only free animals constitute ordinary game or partially protected animals for purposes of Ordinance 84.045 of 1984.[27]

Any party (be it an individual, a company, a not-for-profit organization, or a research institution) seeking to export partially protected or unprotected animals must (a) provide a formal written declaration stating that exportation is not being undertaken for profit and that the animal will be donated to a zoo if the party is required to relinquish it; (b) obtain an exportation authorization issued by the Directorate of Waters, Forests and Hunting; (c) obtain a Sanitary Certificate issued by the Directorate of Breeding; and (d) pay a "special tax for the exportation of live animals."[28]

The eggs of birds and reptiles are considered as live animals.[29]

D. Hunting Permits and Licenses

Hunting is allowed only pursuant to customary hunting rights or to a valid hunting permit.[30] Different types of hunting permits are issued depending on the beneficiary of the permit and type of animal involved.[31] Some of the restrictions imposed by hunting permits are: (a) only adult males of each species may be hunted;[32] (b) regardless of the type of hunting permit issued, no more than two mammals of the same species and no more than four distinct species of mammals may be killed on the same day;[33] and (c) no more than ten mammals may be killed within the same week.[34] The Ministry of the Interior may grant Central African citizens supplementary permits to hunt under more favorable conditions.[35] Holders of hunting permits enjoy free ownership over the skins of their authorized hunt.[36]

The capture of the wild animals included in Annex 2, Lists B and C, of Ordinance 84.045 of 1984[37] concerning the Protection of Wildlife and Regulating Hunting[38] may be undertaken

---

[27] Ordinance 84.045 of 1984, art. 31.

[28] Law 61/281 of 1961, art. 17.

[29] Ordinance 84.062 of 1984, art. 10.

[30] Ordinance 84.045 of 1984, art. 34.

[31] *Id.* arts. 40–43.

[32] *Id.* art. 58.

[33] *Id.* art. 59.

[34] *Id.* art. 60.

[35] *Id.* arts. 44–45.

[36] Law 61/281 of 1961, art. 5.

[37] Annex II, List A of Ordinance 84.045 of 1984 includes, among others, the following animals: leopards, cheetas, gorillas, chimpanzees, rhinoceroses, jackals. Annex II, List B of Ordinance 84.045 of 1984 includes, among others, the following animals: lions, servals (a type of wildcat), elephants, buffaloes. Finally, Annex II, List

only by the governmental agency in charge of wildlife, or by an organ under its control; in all other cases a capture permit is required.[39] The Council of Ministers may, by decree, forbid permanently or temporarily, the capture of these animals in specific areas.[40] The capture of fully protected animals for noncommercial purposes[41] may exceptionally be undertaken with the express authorization of the Chief of State with the advice of the High Commissioner for Wildlife.[42]

Ordinance 84.062 of 1984 regulates the capture and exportation of live wild animals for scientific or commercial purposes.[43] The High Commissioner in charge of wildlife approves permits for the commercial capture of live wild animals to national or foreign individuals or organizations.[44]

The Ministries of Agriculture; Breeding; Waters and Forests; and Tourism issue commercial capture permits by joint decree; permit holders must pay a patent fee, and a "special tax for the exportation of live animals"; the permit authorizes the capture of unprotected animals without any limitations.[45]

The exportation of live wild animals from the national territory requires a certificate of origin and an exportation permit issued by the Hunting Directorate, as well as a sanitary certificate issued by the Breeding Service, and the payment of a special exportation tax.[46] The exportation of spoils and trophies must be made pursuant to a Certificate of Origin issued by the Directorate of Waters, Forests and Hunting, and a Sanitary Certificate issued by the Directorate of Breeding.[47]

The Ministry of Waters and Forests may issue professional identity cards for hunting guides.[48] Identity cards are nontransferable.[49]

C of Ordinance 84.045 of 1984 includes, among others, the following animals: mangabeys (an arboreal African monkey), cercocebus, horses, francolins, and hares.

[38] *See* Ordinance 84.045 of 1984, art. 27.

[39] Ordinance 84.062 of 1984, art. 3.

[40] *Id.* art. 5.

[41] Those animals are listed in Annex 2, List A, of Ordinance 84.045 of 1984.

[42] Ordinance 84.062 of 1984, art. 4.

[43] *Id.* arts. 1, 2.

[44] Decree 84.341 of 1984, art. 3.

[45] Law 61/281 of 1961, art. 2.

[46] The Centre National pour la Protection de la Fauna [National Center for the Protection and Management of Wildlife, CNPAF] collects the special tax on the exportation of live wild animals. Ordinance 84.062 of 1984, arts. 9, 11. A Decree of the Council of Ministers determines the tax rates for hunting permits. Ordinance 84.045 of 1984, art. 47.

[47] Law 61/281 of 1961, art. 4.

[48] Decree 0633 of 1972, art. 3.

[49] *Id.* art. 6.

II. Crimes Related to Poaching and Trafficking in Wildlife

A. General Criminal Activities

Absent a duly issued hunting permit as established in Section 1 D above, the following activities are forbidden: (a) all hunting acts[50] that involve the killing, injuring, capturing, disturbing, or scaring of wild animals or their environment;[51] (b) the introduction, possession and use of hunting spears, with the exception of defense spears;[52] (c) hunting by means of certain instruments and procedures;[53] and (d) possession or transfer of spoils or trophies of fully protected animals included in List A of Annex 2.[54]

Spoils or trophies of partially protected animals included in List B of Annex 2 may not be held, transferred, or exported without a certificate of origin and an export permit,[55] while that of ordinary game included in List C of Annex 2 is permitted.[56]

With regard to herders, the following activities are forbidden to those authorized to stay temporarily within the autonomous territory of Birao and within zones of hunting interest, be they owners, breeders, drivers, conveyors of herds, or those accompanying them:[57] (a) the introduction, possession, or use of more than one lance per herder; (b) the introduction, transportation, and use of hunting netting; (c) the introduction, possession, or use of all bows and arrows; and (d) the introduction and use of horses, with the exception of prestige horses at a maximum of one horse per herd.

B. Criminal Offenses Concerning Elephants and Ivory

Elephant hunting is forbidden throughout the entire territory of the Central African Republic.[58] The collection and commercialization of ivory within national parks and wildlife reserves is absolutely forbidden.[59] However, hunters who legally kill an elephant have the rights to its tusks,[60] and may freely collect, sell, or export them from the national territory[61] in

---

[50] A hunting act is "any act aimed at killing, injuring, or capturing game." Ordinance 84.045 of 1984, art. 33. Ordinance 84.045 of 1984, art. 33 also provides that the carrying of hunting weapons or machines under the conditions established therein constitutes a hunting act. *Id.*

[51] *Id.* art. 5.

[52] Decree 62-239 of 1962, art. 1.

[53] Ordinance 84.045 of 1984, arts. 61–63.

[54] *Id.* art. 78.

[55] *Id.* art. 80.

[56] *Id.* art. 79.

[57] Law 60-126 of 1960, art. 1.

[58] Ordinance 85.005 of 1985, art. 1.

[59] Ordinance 81-013 of 1981, art. 3.

[60] Ordinance 84.045 of 1984, art. 81.

[61] *Id.* art. 84.

accordance with Ordinance 81-013 of 1981.[62] For all these transactions, a Certificate of Origin is required,[63] and certificates must be issued" by duly authorized organizations.[64]

The transformation of ivory may be performed only in accordance with the requirements established in a decree issued jointly by the Ministry of Hunting and the Ministry of Commerce and Industry.[65] Collectors and ivory sales officers may operate only after paying a patent and a tax.[66] The exportation of ivory is subject to taxes,[67] and may take place only under the control of the Customs Service through legally authorized organizations using international airlines departing from the national airport.[68]

Ivory or spoils proceeding from confiscations resulting from violations of legislation related to hunting are sent to the Conservator of Land Property,[69] for public sale to the benefit of the state.[70]

III. Penalties

The cutting, mutilation, pruning, or tearing off of either species within an integral natural reserve or protected species without a special authorization is punishable by imprisonment from one to five years and/or a fine from 200,000 to 1 million francs (about US$400 to $2,000).[71]

Anyone hunting without a valid permit, hunting outside the restrictions established in permit, or failing to submit the slaughter report required by legislation[72] is subject to imprisonment from one to six months and/or a fine from 100 to 300 francs (about US$.20 to $.60), without prejudice to the taxes due according to the applicable legislation.[73]

Ordinance 84.045 of 1984[74] describes punishable activities and establishes different jail terms and pecuniary penalties for specific acts. Violations of Ordinance 84.062 of 1984 are punishable in accordance with articles 105 to 120 of Ordinance 84.045 of 1984.[75] Violations of

---

[62] Ordinance 81-013 of 1981, art. 2.

[63] *Id.* art. 5.

[64] Ordinance 84.045 of 1984, art. 88; Ordinance 81-013 of 1981, art. 6.

[65] Ordinance 81-013 of 1981, art. 9.

[66] *Id.* art. 10.

[67] *Id.* art. 12.

[68] *Id.* art. 13.

[69] Law 61/281 of 1961, art. 8.

[70] *Id.* art. 9.

[71] Forestry Code of 2008, art. 96.

[72] Ordinance 84.045 of 1984

[73] *Id.* art. 106.

[74] *Id.* arts. 107-120.

[75] *Id.* art. 13.

Law 62/350 of 1963 are punishable with fines and/or imprisonment, without prejudice to the seizure of the instruments and effects involved in the offense.[76] Arts. 5 to 8 list about seven specific acts that are punished, including false declarations, failure to observe sanitary measures, and fraudulent use of permits.

Any violation of Ordinance 81-013 of 1981 concerning ivory is punishable with a fine of 1 to 5 million francs (about US$2,000 to $10,000) and/or imprisonment from two to five years, without prejudice to the confiscation of the instruments and effects of the offense.[77]

Instruments and materials utilized to commit the offenses as well as their products are confiscated for the benefit of the State.[78]

IV. Enforcement Authorities

In the Central African Republic, the enforcement of hunting rules and environmental protection legislation is delegated to specific government agencies in accordance with their responsibilities, as follows:

- Enforcement of Ordinance 84.062 of 1984 lies with the Ministry of National Defense, the Ministry of Rural Development, the Ministry of the Interior, and the High Commissioner for Tourism, Waters, Forests, Hunting, and Fishing.[79]

- Enforcement of Ordinance 84.045 of 1984[80] lies with (a) officers and agents of the judicial police; (b) sworn officers of the Administration of Waters, Forests, Hunting, and Fishing; (c) sworn hunting guides; and (d) park and reserve rangers.

- Enforcement of Decree 84.341 of 1984 lies with the Ministry of Economy and Finances, and the High Commissioner for Tourism, Waters, Forests, Hunting, and Fishing.[81]

- Enforcement of Ordinance 81-013 of 1981 concerning ivory lies with the Ministry of Hunting, the Ministry of Commerce and Industry, the Ministry of Finance, the Ministry of National Defense, and the Ministry of Justice.[82]

- Enforcement of Law 62/350 of 1963 lies with the Ministry of Agriculture[83] and the Plant Protection Service.[84]

---

[76] Law 62/350 of 1963, arts. 5–8.

[77] Ordinance 81-013 of 1981, art. 16.

[78] Forestry Code of 2008, art. 102.

[79] Ordinance 84.062 of 1984, art. 14.

[80] Ordinance 84.045 of 1984, art. 122.

[81] Decree 84.341 of 1984, art. 8.

[82] Ordinance 81-013 of 1981, art. 17.

[83] Law 62/350 of 1963, art. 4.

[84] *Id.* art. 5.

All of these enforcement officers have the power to seize and confiscate weapons, machines, or vehicles utilized during the commission of these offenses, and the meats, spoils, and trophies of animals illegally captured or killed. Prosecution of these offenses lies with the Attorney General's Office.[85]

Prepared by Dante Figueroa
Senior Legal Information Analyst
January 2013

---

[85] Ordinance 84.045 of 1984, art. 129.

LAW LIBRARY OF CONGRESS

THE DEMOCRATIC REPUBLIC OF THE CONGO

WILDLIFE TRAFFICKING AND POACHING

Executive Summary

The Democratic Republic of the Congo (DRC) has in place a comprehensive legislative framework that criminalizes poaching; dealing in illegal trophies; and importing, exporting, and transferring trophies in violation of substantive and procedural legal requirements. The framework includes penalties for the violation of these provisions, consisting of fines, prison terms, and forfeiture of the instruments and effects used in the course of committing the crimes. Several government agencies share enforcement powers and, in some cases, citizens' organizations are permitted to collaborate with government agencies in the performance of their enforcement duties.

I. Introduction

The Constitution of the Democratic Republic of the Congo[1] reserves for the central government the regulation of hunting, fishing, and the capture of wild animals.[2] However, Congolese provinces retain exclusive jurisdiction in applying national legislation concerning these activities.[3]

The legislation that directly protects wildlife and concerns poaching and illegal trafficking in the DRC includes the Hunting Law of 1982[4] and its implementing Decree 014 of 2004;[5] Law 48 of 1983 on the Conservation and Exploitation of Wildlife;[6] Law 003 of 1991 on

---

[1] The Constitution of the Democratic Republic of the Congo, 2005, *available at* http:// www.constitution net.org/files/DRC%20-%20Congo%20Constitution.pdf.

[2] *Id.* art. 202(25).

[3] *Id.* art. 204(20).

[4] Loi N° 82-002 du 28 mai 1982 portant réglementation de la chasse [Law No. 82-002 of May 28, 1982, on Hunting Regulations (hereinafter Law No. 82-002)], JOURNAL OFFICIEL [J.O.] No. 11, June 11, 1982, *available at* http://faolex fao.org/docs/pdf/cng4275.pdf.

[5] Arrêté N°014/Cab/Min/Env/2004 du 29 Avril 2004 Relatif aux Mesures d'Execution de la Loi N°82-002 du 28 Mai 1982 portant Reglementation de la Chasse [Decree No. 014 of April 29, 2004, Concerning Measures for the Implementation of Law No. 82-002 of May, 1982, Related to the Regulation of Hunting (hereinafter Decree No. 014)], *available at* http://www.leganet.cd/Legislation/Droit%20economique/Chasse/A041.29.04.2004 htm.

[6] Loi N° 48/83 du 21 avril 1983 définissant les Conditions de la Conservation et de l'Exploitation de la Faune Sauvage [Law No. 48/83 of April 21, 1983, Defining the Conditions of the Conservation and Exploitation of Wildlife (hereinafter Law No. 48/83)], *available at* http://www.cesbc.org/congo/Lois/Loi%2048-83%20du%2021%20avril%201983.pdf.

the Protection of the Environment;[7] the Criminal Code of 2004;[8] and Law 37 of 2008 on Wildlife and Protected Areas.[9] This legislation defines hunting as any act aimed at capturing or killing animals regardless of their protection status.[10] The Law makes it irrelevant whether a hunter has intent to take ownership of all or part of the trophy or skins,[11] and recognizes as an act of capture any action aimed at depriving those animals of their freedom or collecting the eggs of birds or reptiles from their hatching place.[12]

The skins, meat and eggs of animals that have been shot dead or captured alive are considered hunting products.[13] Hunting products also include the tusks of elephants, horns of rhinoceros, and teeth of hippopotamus found dead or shot, as well as hunting products collected following an act of legitimate defense against the animal.[14]

II. General Legal Framework for Protecting Wildlife

A. Restricted Areas and Periods

Legislation protecting wildlife restricts the areas in which hunting is permissible, the number of animals that can be hunted, and the means that can be employed in hunting.[15] Hunting activities within hunting zones are subordinated to the potential of the wildlife and the plan for their development and management.[16]

Protected areas are defined as "any natural space covered by specific measures especially destined to sustainably protect and manage biological diversity, in particular: national parks, integral natural reserves, wildlife reserves, special reserves or wildlife sanctuaries, and hunting zones.[17] Protected areas are placed under the control of the State.[18] The Ministry of the

---

[7] Loi No.003/91 du 23 Avril 1991 sur la protection de l'Environnement [Law No. 003/91 of April 23, 1991, Concerning the Protection of the Environment (hereinafter Law No. 003/91)], *available at* http://faolex.fao. org/docs/%20texts/con5810.doc.

[8] CODE PÉNAL CONGOLAIS [CONGOLESE CRIMINAL CODE], J.O. No. Spécial, Nov. 30, 2004, *available at* http://www.ilo.org/dyn/natlex/docs/SERIAL/69343/69050/F279894825/Code%20penal%20 (a%20jour%202004).pdf.

[9] Loi 37-2008 du 28 Novembre 2008 sur la faune et les aires protégées [Law No. 37-2008 of November 28, 2008, Concerning Wildlife and Protected Areas (hereinafter Law No. 37-2008)], J.O., Dec. 4, 2008, *available at* http://faolex.fao.org/docs/pdf/con86726.pdf.

[10] Law No. 48/83, art. 5.

[11] *Id.*

[12] *Id.* art. 6.

[13] Law No. 82-002, art. 73.

[14] *Id.* art. 74.

[15] Law No. 48/83, art. 36.

[16] Law No. 37-2008, art. 16.

[17] *Id.* art. 5.

[18] *Id.* art. 9.

Environment and the Ministry of Forest Economy may create protected areas for the conservation and rational management of fauna and flora.[19] Hunting is prohibited in the reserves defined in Law 48 of 1983, unless the administrative act creating the reserves establishes an exception.[20]

Except by prior authorization from the Ministry of the Environment and the Ministry of Forest Economy for scientific or administrative purposes,[21] the following activities are forbidden in protected areas: (a) hunting, fishing, grazing, and the introduction of endemic animals and vegetables;[22] (b) bushfires, brushfires, and the logging of wood and other plants;[23] (c) the carrying of firearms, or hunting within protected areas;[24] (d) the shooting, hunting, or capturing of protected wildlife, or destruction of their habitat; (e) the destruction, mutilation, extraction, or incineration of protected flora; (f) the exportation of protected species;[25] and (g) the shooting and capture of wild animals within wildlife reserves.[26]

Wildlife reserves or hunting areas are created through a Decree of the Council of Ministers,[27] which authorizes hunting in them only for scientific purposes.[28] Certain partial wildlife areas may be leased to tourism companies or professional hunting associations.[29] Hunting within urban areas is also forbidden and may not take place on lands under concession without the consent of the holder.[30]

The Waters and Forest Agency may establish annual hunting seasons[31] throughout the national territory.[32] Annual hunting periods not exceeding six months are allowed in the regions located north and south of the Equator.[33]

---

[19] Law No. 003/91, art. 11.

[20] Law No. 48/83, art. 8.

[21] Law No. 003/91, art. 20.

[22] Law No. 37-2008, art. 13.

[23] Law No. 003/91, art. 15.

[24] Law No. 37-2008, art. 17.

[25] Law No. 003/91, art. 19.

[26] Law No. 37-2008, art. 14.

[27] *Id.* art. 6.

[28] Law No. 82-002, art. 12.

[29] *Id.* art. 17.

[30] Law No. 48/83, art. 9.

[31] Law No. 37-2008, art. 35.

[32] Law No. 48/83, art. 37.

[33] Law No. 82-002, art. 18.

B. Classification of Wildlife for Regulatory Purposes

All wild animals susceptible to generating a touristic interest or being exploited for their meat, skin, feathers, or trophies[34] belong to the State.[35]

Wild animals are classified in three categories: fully protected, partially protected, and not protected.[36] Decree 014 of 2004, implementing the Hunting Law, contains three annexes on fully, partially, and non-protected flora and fauna.

Fully protected animals may only be disturbed, chased, captured, injured, or killed pursuant to a scientific permit;[37] legitimate defense is inadmissible in these cases.[38]

Partially protected animals may only be hunted pursuant to a sport permit for big game, a grand permit for tourism, or special permits under the conditions established by the hunting authorities.[39]

Non-protected species are regulated by the respective legal instruments.[40]

C. Hunting Permits and Licenses

The importation, exportation, possession, and transport in the national territory of fully protected species and their trophies or skins, are forbidden.[41] The Waters and Forests Agency (Bureau des Eaux et Forêts) may grant permits[42] for purposes of scientific research or animal reproduction[43] or an authorization for their exportation in accordance with international conventions.[44] The Waters and Forests Agency may reject the issuance of a hunting permit or license on the grounds of public policy.[45] Hunting permits and licenses are granted by decree.[46]

---

[34] "Trophy" is defined as "any specimen or part of a dead animal." Law No. 48/83, art. 34.

[35] *Id.* art. 1.

[36] Law No. 82-002, arts. 26-33; Law No. 48/83, art. 2; and Law No. 37-2008, art. 24.

[37] *Id.* art. 27.

[38] *Id.* art. 28.

[39] *Id.* art. 31.

[40] Law No. 37-2008, art. 29.

[41] *Id.* art. 27.

[42] Law No. 82-002, arts. 4–7; Law No. 37-2008, art. 39 (stating that the exploitation of wildlife through hunting activities may only be performed pursuant to a prior hunting authorization issued by the competent authority).

[43] Law No. 37-2008, art. 27.

[44] *Id.* art. 30.

[45] Law No. 48/83, art. 10.

[46] *Id.* art. 11.

No person may engage in hunting activities without holding a permit or license and without submitting to the authority of the place where the hunting activities are intended.[47] A hunting permit is also necessary to hunt by certain special means mentioned in the law, inter alia, automatic weapons, poison and toxic products.[48]

There are three basic types of hunting permits established by the Law on the Conservation and Exploitation of Wildlife of 1983. They are sport permits, scientific permits, and special possession permits.[49] The Law 37 of 2008 on Wildlife and Protected Areas expanded this list and provided for two additional types of permits such as village hunting or harvest permits, and collection permits.[50] The last two are aimed at regulating traditional hunting carried out by rural populations to satisfy their individual and communal needs within their territories or within zones open to traditional hunting.[51]

Individuals involved in varied hunting related activities shall possess licenses issued by local authorities. Legislation specifies licenses for hunting guides, farming and capture of crocodiles and lizards, and for professional photographers of wild animals,[52] commercial capture of animals, game farming, and game ranches.[53] Sport and scientific permits as well as commercial capture licenses require prior liability insurance.[54]

There are common provisions to permits and licenses: (a) all their conditions are established in the respective decree;[55] (b) they are personal and non-transferable[56] under any circumstances, whether for profit or not;[57] (c) they are contingent on being adapted to the development of animal populations;[58] (d) they may be granted only to those abiding by the applicable regulations related to firearms permits (including annual firearm taxes),[59] hunting, and the protection of wildlife;[60] (e) they are valid for one calendar year; (f) applicants for permits and licenses must obtain unlimited insurance for accidents involving third parties;[61] and (g) all

---

[47] *Id.* art. 7.

[48] Law No. 82-002, art. 21.

[49] Law No. 48/83, art. 12.

[50] Law No. 37-2008, art. 41.

[51] *Id.* art. 62.

[52] Law No. 48/83, art. 13.

[53] Law No. 37-2008, art. 42.

[54] *Id.* art. 43.

[55] Law No. 48/83, art. 16.

[56] Law No. 82-002, art. 37; Law No. 37-2008, art. 40.

[57] Law No. 48/83, art. 14.

[58] *Id.* art. 15.

[59] *Id.* art. 22.

[60] *Id.* art. 18.

[61] Law No. 48/83, art. 20.

applicants for a sport permit or a license must declare that they know the applicable legislation, will fulfill the conditions for obtaining the permit or license, and accept that any false declaration will result in the withdrawal of the permit or license without prejudice of other penalties established by law.[62]

Commercial capture permits do not allow the use of firearms and may not be granted for fully protected animals.[63] The importation, exportation, re-exportation, and transport of partially protected species and their trophies may be authorized by decree of the Council of Ministers.[64] Additionally, the exportation of a fully or partially protected animal must be made pursuant to a Legitimate Detention Certificate[65] and previous payment of the applicable taxes.[66]

Sport hunting permits apply only to male animals and, with a few exceptions, the hunting of females and the young is prohibited; hunting of female mammals with calves is forbidden.[67] Except for scientific purposes, the hunting of newborns, the young, females with calves, and nesting birds and reptiles is forbidden.[68]

Taxes may be imposed on any form of exploitation of products from wildlife.[69] The Law specifies that the issuance of scientific hunting permits is subject to taxes.[70]

III. Crimes Related to Poaching and Trafficking in Wildlife

The following hunting activities are strictly forbidden: (a) hunting at night;[71] (b) shooting a wild animal from a motor vehicle, vessel, or aircraft;[72] (c) the use of hunting techniques, methods or instruments causing unnecessary suffering to animals or damaging their environment;[73] (d) prejudicial manipulations of wild animals;[74] (e) hunting on public roads,

---

[62] *Id.* art. 24.

[63] Law No. 82-002, arts. 27, 28 & 68.

[64] Law No. 37-2008, art. 28.

[65] Law No. 82-002, art. 71.

[66] *Id.* art. 72.

[67] Law No. 48/83, art. 38.

[68] Law No. 37-2008, art. 32.

[69] *Id.* art. 73.

[70] Law No. 82-002, art. 64.

[71] Law No. 37-2008, art. 36.

[72] *Id.* art. 36.

[73] *Id.* art. 37.

[74] *Id.* art. 33.

railways, and airfields;[75] (f) systematic hunting of young animals and the removal of eggs;[76] and (g) the shooting of elephants with tusks weighing 5 kilograms or lower.[77]

The following activities are forbidden in wildlife reserves: (a) introducing domestic or exotic animals, firearms, traps, or any hunting weapons;[78] (b) chasing, hunting, capturing, destroying, scaring, or disturbing any wild animal except in the case of legitimate defense[79] or force majeure;[80] (c) causing irreversible deterioration of wildlife habitat;[81] and (d) flying aircraft at an altitude lower than 500 meters.[82]

Anyone who injures an animal is required to make every effort to locate and dispatch it, unless the animal enters a protected area. If the hunter has not dispatched the animal in concern and it is a gorilla, chimpanzee, elephant, buffalo, lion, or hippopotamus, a detailed statement must be provided, under the penalty of judicial prosecution by the Waters and Forests Agency.[83]

Offenses to the law are classified as crimes and infringements.[84]

The following activities, among others, constitute crimes for purposes of Law 48 of 1983:[85] (a) the illicit hunting of fully or partially protected animals; (b) the use of scientific permits for commercial purposes; (c) operating as a hunting guide without a license; (d) the capture of wild animals and the possession of their products without a scientific permit or license; (e) the hunting of crocodiles or lizards without a license; and (f) trading in tusks and the skin of crocodiles and lizards without a license.

The following activities constitute infringements for purposes of Law 48 of 1983:[86] (a) the failure to submit a slaughter declaration within the term established in the law; (b) hunting outside the territory allowed by the respective permit; (c) unauthorized hunting within authorized territories; (d) hunting of partially protected animals with traditional instruments; (e) grazing or herding livestock within classified areas; (f) the removal of eggs; and (f) the extraction or sampling of any products or samples within the limits of a classified area.

---

[75] Law No. 82-002, art. 16.

[76] Law No. 48/83, art. 39.

[77] *Id.* art. 40.

[78] Law No. 82-002, art. 13(1).

[79] *Id.* arts. 83–84.

[80] *Id.* art. 13(2).

[81] *Id.* art. 13(3).

[82] *Id.* art. 13(4).

[83] *Id.* art. 27.

[84] *Id.* art. 48.

[85] *Id.* art. 49.

[86] *Id.* art. 50.

Hunting guides are responsible for all offenses committed by their clients during a hunting expedition organized or guided by them.[87]

IV. Penalties

All violations of the law related to the protection of flora and fauna or of measures aimed at its enforcement are punishable with either imprisonment for up to five years or a fine of 5 to 50,000 zaires.

Perpetrators of and accomplices to the crimes described in Law 48 of 1983 are punished with either fines (10,000 to 10 million francs) or imprisonment (two months to five years) or both.[88] In the case of recidivism the maximum penalty is applied conjointly with the withdrawal of the permit or license. The judge may also order the confiscation of the instruments and effects of the crimes and the temporal or definitive termination of the permit or license.[89]

Perpetrators and accomplices of the infringements described in Law 48 of 1983 are punished with either fines (5,000 to 5 million francs) or imprisonment or both.[90]

Penalties are doubled in the case of the violation of restricted hunting areas or periods,[91] or if the action is committed in a wildlife reserve, hunting area, or national park; by a government agent or person in charge of a hunting mission; or in the case of recidivism.[92]

Legislation establishes presumptions of guilt: (a) anyone found in possession of a fully or partially protected animal, dead or alive, is presumed to have captured or killed the animal himself;[93] (b) anyone found at night outside of urban areas in possession of a hunting weapon and a frontal lamp or a lamp that has been modified to be fixed to the head or hair is presumed to have hunted with the aid of an illuminating device;[94] (c) anyone caught in the act of hunting without a proper permit (i.e., poaching) is presumed to have committed the crime and shall pay triple the tax established for obtaining the respective permit, without prejudice of other criminal penalties;[95] (d) anyone found in possession of weapons and firearms, lights, and other instruments in specified areas is presumed to be hunting illegally;[96] and (e) anyone found in possession of a live or dead animal that is fully, partially, or nonprotected or of any part thereof is presumed to have captured or killed the animal, and thus to have violated applicable

---

[87] Decree No. 014, art. 63.

[88] Law No. 48/83, art. 60.

[89] *Id.* arts. 62 & 66.

[90] *Id.* art. 61.

[91] Law No. 82-002, arts. 18 & 19.

[92] *Id.* art. 85.

[93] *Id.* art. 86.

[94] *Id.* art. 86.

[95] *Id.* art. 87.

[96] Law No. 48/83, art. 79.

legislation. These are rebuttable presumptions, and the suspect may prove his innocence by providing a legal title to the animal or part thereof.[97] No penalties apply to those who perform an illegal hunting act under the immediate necessity of defense of self, of another, or of one's own domestic livestock.[98] If during the exercise of a user's right, a protected animal is shot, a declaration must be made to the local authority, the failure to do which is a violation of the law.[99]

Enforcement activities include: (a) collecting fines, making restitutions, and awarding damages;[100] (b) confiscating all hunting products sold or illegally trafficked as well as all illicit hunting instruments utilized;[101] and (c) the withdrawal of permits and licenses.[102] Enforcement officers exercise broad powers of inspection, seizure, confiscation, and arrest.[103]

The following elements are subject to seizure and confiscation: (a) weapons, munitions, and instruments utilized to violate any provisions of this Law, in addition to animal carcasses produced through illegal hunting;[104] and (b) means of transportation utilized in illegal hunting.[105] All the fruits of confiscations are property of the State; confiscated war weapons will be sent to the People's National Army Chiefs of Staff.[106]

Imprisonment and fines are imposed according to the nature of the offense without prejudice of seizure, confiscation, and withdrawal of permits and licenses.[107] The maximum penalties are imposed under the following conditions:[108] (a) when a fully protected animal is slaughtered; (b) when the perpetrator is an agent of the government or of a territorial collectivity;[109] (c) when the violation is committed during a closed season; and (d) in case of recidivism. First-time offenders may request in lieu of prison terms and fines the performance of mandatory public service aimed at the conservation of wildlife, natural habitats, protected areas, and natural environments for the reproduction and migration of wild animals.[110]

---

[97] *Id.* art. 54.

[98] *Id.* art. 31.

[99] *Id.* art. 33.

[100] *Id.* art. 52.

[101] *Id.* art. 53.

[102] *Id.* art. 59.

[103] *Id.* art. 53.

[104] Law No. 37-2008, art. 110.

[105] *Id.* art. 111.

[106] Law No. 48/83, arts. 66, 68–70 & 85.

[107] Law No. 37-2008, arts. 112 & 113.

[108] *Id.* art. 114.

[109] Law No. 48/83, art. 65.

[110] Law No. 37-2008, art. 115.

The Criminal Code of 2004 punishes with imprisonment for two months to ten years and/or a fine of 25 to 300 zaïres those who maliciously and unnecessarily kill or seriously injure cattle or domestic animals belonging to others.[111]

There is a three-year statute of limitations on tort liability arising from the violation of the provisions of this Law.[112]

V. Enforcement Authorities

Those designated as enforcement authorities vary among all the pieces of legislation regulating wildlife.

The Hunting Law of 1982, for example, provides that a specialized government agency may be created for the management of hunting activities.[113] Decree 014 of 2004, in turn, states that the responsibility for enforcement rests with the Waters and Forests Agency and the Congolese Institute for the Conservation of Nature (Institut Congolais pour la Conservation de la Nature).[114] The Agency's Director and its regional chiefs act as judicial police officers.[115] The Hunting Police and the Ministry of Bailiffs also collaborate in enforcement,[116] as do eco-guards, whose legal existence has been approved by decree of the Council of Ministers.[117] Additionally, village chiefs and pertinent local associations also assist the authorities with enforcement responsibilities.[118]

Law 003 of 1991 is enforced by officers from the Ministry of the Environment and the judicial police, in collaboration with officers from the Ministries of Forest Economy, Health, Mining and Energy, Hydraulics, Transportation and Civil Aviation, Public Works and Construction, and with local collectives.[119]

Violations are determined through an oral procedure by agents of the Waters and Forests Agency or of other authorized agencies established in article 48 of Law 004/74 of January 4, 1974.[120]

The Attorney General files criminal actions for violations concerning wildlife and hunting[121] in accordance with the Code of Criminal Procedure.[122] Jurisdiction over crimes and

---

[111] Law No. 003/91, art. 114.

[112] Law No. 48/83, art. 73.

[113] Law No. 82-002, arts. 8 & 9.

[114] Decree No. 014, art. 69.

[115] Law No. 82-002, arts. 10 & 11; Law No. 48/83, art. 51.

[116] Law No. 48/83, art. 74.

[117] Law No. 37-2008, art. 96.

[118] *Id.* art. 95.

[119] Law No. 003/91, art. 67.

[120] Law No. 48/83, art. 51.

infringements as well as over wildlife protection lies with the Courts of First Instance and High Courts.[123]   The Minister of Waters and Forests, the General Director, and the Provincial Directors of Waters and Forests may settle cases involving violations concerning wildlife and hunting for an amount of up to 5 million francs; no settlement is allowed in the case of recidivism.[124]

VI. International Conventions

The DRC is a signatory to the Convention on International Trade in Endangered Species of Wild Fauna and Flora (CITES),[125] which took effect in the DRC in 1983.[126]

Prepared by Dante Figueroa
Senior Legal Information Analyst
January 2013

---

[121] Law No. 37-2008, art. 102.

[122] *Id.* art. 104.

[123] Law No. 48/83, art. 78.

[124] Law No. 37-2008, art. 106.

[125] Convention on International Trade in Endangered Species of Wild Fauna and Flora, Mar. 3, 1973, 993 U.N.T.S. 243, http://www.cites.org/eng/disc/text.php.

[126] *List of Contracting Parties*, CITES, http://www.cites.org/eng/disc/parties/alphabet.php (last visited Jan. 16, 2013).

LAW LIBRARY OF CONGRESS

KENYA

WILDLIFE TRAFFICKING AND POACHING

Executive Summary

Kenya has in place a comprehensive legislative framework that criminalizes not only wildlife poaching but also importing, exporting, dealing in, and transferring illegal animal trophies. Penalties for violations of the substantive laws and required legal procedures consist of fines, prison terms, and forfeiture of tools used in committing a crime, as well as the fruits of the crime themselves.

While certain aspects of enforcing the substantive laws are shared across several government institutions, it is the Kenya Wildlife Service (KWS), an institution with full prosecutorial powers, that bears the primary responsibility for wildlife law enforcement.

I. Introduction

The Wildlife (Conservation and Management) Act of 1976 (WCMA) is a comprehensive piece of legislation criminalizing the hunting of protected animals and the unlicensed hunting of game.[1] This law also prohibits various other acts, which include importing or exporting a trophy[2] without proper permission, dealing in trophies without a license, and transfer of trophies in disregard of legal procedures for proper transfer of ownership.

The task of enforcing the law is a responsibility shared across various law enforcement institutions. Among the government agents that can enforce this law are officers of the Kenya Wildlife Service (KWS), forest officers, police officers, and administrative officers. However, the principal enforcement agency is the Kenya Wildlife Service (KWS), which has a Security Division that investigates wildlife crimes, among other things, and has prosecutorial powers.

---

[1] Wildlife (Conservation and Management) Act of 1976, 15 LAWS OF KENYA, Cap. 376 (rev. ed. 2009), available at the Kenyan Law Reports website, http://www.kenyalaw.org/klr/fileadmin/pdfdownloads/Acts/Wildlife_Conservation_and_Management_Act__Cap_376_.pdf.

[2] A "trophy" is defined as "any protected animal, game animal, or game bird, alive or dead and any bone, claw, egg, feather, hair, hoof, skin, tooth, tusk or other durable portion whatsoever of that animal or bird or fish or other aquatic life whether processed, added to or changed by the work of man or not, which is recognizable as such a durable portion." *Id.* § 2.

It is worth noting that the Cabinet recently proposed a bill to repeal and replace the existing legislation, which if adopted would provide for a comprehensive institutional framework and impose more stringent penalties for wildlife offenses.[3]

II. Poaching and Trafficking in Wildlife

The WCMA establishes three different conditions under which hunting is criminalized. First, hunting certain classes of animals is a crime. The law prohibits the hunting of a protected animal[4] as well as the hunting of a game animal[5] without a proper license or in violation of the terms of a license.[6] A person who violates this provision commits what is known as a "forfeiture offence."[7] A person who hunts a game bird without a license or in violation of the terms of a license commits an "offence."[8]

The law also imposes prohibitions on hunting in certain places. A person who hunts any animal (protected animal, game animal, or otherwise) in a national park or national reserve is subject to penalties for a forfeiture offense, as well as to other specific penalties.[9] The law also makes hunting any animal in a local sanctuary or area designated as such by a competent authority a forfeiture offense.[10]

Finally, the law imposes strict prohibitions on the use of certain tools and methods of hunting, mainly those giving a licensed hunter undue advantage over his prey. These include

- using certain types of gin or other similar traps, fire, automatic weapons, explosives, and poisoned weapons;

- hunting a game animal between dusk and dawn;

- engaging in a game drive other than a drive of birds;

- driving a game animal into water to capture, incapacitate or kill it;

- using certain vehicles and communication gear to facilitate the hunting of a game animal.[11]

---

[3] The Wildlife Bill, 2011, *available at* the Kenya Wildlife Service website, http://www.kws.org/export/sites/kws/info/publications/acts_policies/Wildlife-Bill-2011.pdf; *Cabinet Pass [sic] Wildlife and Mineral Bills to Boost Sectors*, COASTWEEK KENYA (Oct. 12–18, 2012), http://www.coastweek.com/3541_minerals.htm; Jill Craig, *Kenya Anti-Poaching Laws May Get Overhaul*, VOICE OF AMERICA (Nov. 29, 2012), http://www.voanews.com/content/kenyas-outdated-wildlife-laws-heading-for-an-overhaul/1555521.html.

[4] Wildlife (Conservation and Management) Act, Third Schedule.

[5] *Id.*, First Schedule.

[6] *Id.* § 22.

[7] *Id.*

[8] *Id.*

[9] *Id.* §§ 13, 18.

[10] *Id.* § 19.

[11] *Id.* §§ 34 & 35.

A person who violates these provisions commits a forfeiture offense.

Besides hunting prohibitions, the law also prohibits dealing in, importing, exporting, and transferring trophies without a proper license or documentation. A person who engages in a dealer's business without the proper license or in violation of the terms of a license commits an offense.[12] A person who transfers a trophy to another without an ownership certificate and/or without endorsing the certificate in the prescribed manner also commits an offense.[13] The law makes it a forfeiture offense to export

- any live animal, game animal, or bird without a proper permit and other than through a customs port entry;

- any trophy other than a live animal without a certificate of ownership and other than through a customs port of entry; and

- any animal or trophy designated as a prohibited export without a permit.[14]

Similarly, it is prohibited to import any trophy, unmanufactured ivory, or rhinoceros horn of any description without informing customs agents at the port of entry and producing it for inspection.[15] Once in Kenya, the importer is required to approach the KWS to register the item(s) and obtain an ownership certificate if one has not already been issued in the country of origin.[16] The law also prohibits importing a trophy designated a prohibited import.[17] A person who violates any of these provisions commits a forfeiture offense and is also subject to other specific penalties not related to those for a forfeiture offense.[18]

III. Penalties

There are two classes of penalties, specific and general. Specific penalties are those stipulated for the violation of a particular legal provision. In the context of the WCMA, a person convicted of hunting any animal in a national park is subject to a fine ranging from 5000 Kenyan shillings (KES) (around US$58) to 20,000 KES (around US$232), and/or imprisonment ranging from six months to three years, which may include corporal punishment.[19] Another good example of a provision imposing specific penalties is the crime of carrying on the business of a dealer without a license or in violation of the terms of one. A person convicted of this crime is

---

[12] *Id.* § 43.

[13] *Id.* § 44.

[14] *Id.* § 45.

[15] *Id.* § 40.

[16] *Id.*

[17] *Id.*

[18] *Id.*

[19] *Id.* §13. While the reference to corporal punishment remains in the WCMA, a provision on corporal punishment for certain crimes under the Kenyan Penal Code was repealed in 2003. The Penal Code § 27, 12 LAWS OF KENYA, Cap. 63 (rev. ed. 2009), *available at* the Kenya Law Reports website, http://www.kenyalaw.org/Downloads/GreyBook/8. %20The%20Penal%20Code.pdf.

subject to a fine of up to 20,000 KES and/or a prison term of up to five years.[20] A person who transfers trophies in violation of the WCMA is, on conviction, subject to a fine of up to 10,000 KES (about US$116) and/or one year imprisonment.[21]

In contrast, four classes of general penalties are imposed under the WCMA, depending on the severity of the offense. First, an offense involving a protected animal, an animal listed in Part I of the First Schedule of the controlling law (an elephant, leopard, lion, or rhinoceros), or the animal's trophy is punishable by a fine of up to 40,000 KES (about US$464) and/or up to ten years in prison.[22] Second, if an offense involves an animal listed in Part II of the First Schedule (a bongo, reticulated giraffe, Rothschild giraffe, Kenya hartebeeste, greater kudu, black-and-white colobus monkey, beisa oryx, fringe-eared oryx, or Grévy's zebra) or the animal's trophy, the applicable penalties are much lower—a fine of up to 20,000 KES (about US$232) and/or a prison term not exceeding five years.[23]

Two types of penalty apply to forfeiture offenses. A forfeiture offense not covered under the above-listed two classes of offenses is punishable by a fine of up to 15,000 KES (US$174) and/or prison term not exceeding three years.[24] In addition, unless the court decides otherwise, the perpetrator forfeits to the government the instruments involved in the commission of the crime and the fruits of the crime.[25]

The fourth class of penalty applies to all other offenses and involves a fine of up to 1000 KES (about US$11) and/or six months imprisonment.[26]

IV. Enforcement Authority

The KWS was established under the WCMA and is a state corporation with the mandate to conserve and manage Kenya's wildlife as well as enforce all the relevant laws.[27] The KWS's Security Division is mandated to protect wildlife and enforce the WCMA.[28]

The Security Division has five departments, including the Wildlife Protection Department, Intelligence Department, and Investigation Department. The Wildlife Protection Department, which in addition to its ranger workforce includes a unit of tracker dogs, combats

---

[20] Wildlife (Conservation and Management) Act § 43.

[21] *Id.* § 44.

[22] *Id.* § 56.

[23] *Id.*

[24] *Id.*

[25] *Id.* § 52.

[26] *Id.* § 56.

[27] *Id.* pt. II; *see also Overview – About Us*, KENYA WILDLIFE SERVICE, http://www.kws.org/about/index.html (last visited Dec. 14, 2012).

[28] *Security Service*, KENYA WILDLIFE SERVICE, http://www.kws.org/about/security.html (last visited Dec. 14, 2012).

poaching.[29]   The Intelligence Department's functions include "surveillance and monitoring of bandits and gangs around wildlife-protected areas."[30]   Finally, the Investigation Department investigates wildlife crimes, including poaching and illegal trophies.[31]   In addition, it has statutorily conferred prosecutorial powers.[32]   The WCMA confers on any of the members of the Department above the rank of a ranger, subject to the supervision by the Attorney-General, all the powers available to a public prosecutor to prosecute any violation of its provisions.[33]

Certain enforcement powers are shared with other government institutions. The WCMA gives any authorized officer (including an officer of the KWS, a forest officer, a police officer or an administrative officer) enforcement powers, which include inspection, detention, arrest, and search-and-seizure powers.[34]

Prepared by Hanibal Goitom
Foreign Law Specialist
November 2012

---

[29] *Id.*

[30] *Id.*

[31] *Id.*

[32] *Id.*; Wildlife (Conservation and Management) Act § 54.

[33] Wildlife (Conservation and Management) Act § 54.

[34] *Id.* § 49.

LAW LIBRARY OF CONGRESS

MOZAMBIQUE

WILDLIFE TRAFFICKING AND POACHING

Executive Summary

Specific laws regulate hunting in Mozambique. Those laws permit hunting in determined areas, require hunters to obtain a license, and protect some animals. Violations of the regulations are punishable with a fine and compensatory measures aimed at repairing the damage caused. The Penal Code punishes with three days in prison and a fine a person who hunts in areas where hunting is not permitted, uses prohibited means, or enters into areas for the purpose of hunting without the consent of the owner. Wildlife trafficking, however, is not criminalized.

Storage or transportation of, or trade in, forest and wildlife resources requires an authorization and must follow the conditions established by law. The Ministry of Agriculture and Rural Development is responsible for the administration, management, and monitoring of activities involving the use of forest and wildlife resources and their ecosystems in the national territory.

I. Legal Framework

In Mozambique, Law No. 10 of July 7, 1999, establishes the principles and basic norms concerning the protection, preservation, and sustainable use of forest and wildlife resources. Law No. 10 is regulated by Decree No. 12 of June 6, 2002. The Penal Code criminalizes hunting activities that are not in accordance with hunting regulations.

A. Law No. 10 of July 7, 1999

Article 6 of Law No. 10 determines that the wildlife patrimony comprises the existing wildlife in the country and is classified according to its rarity and cultural and socioeconomic value through lists of species to be established by statute.[1]

Article 20 defines the categories for the exploitation of wildlife in the country, which consist of a simple hunting license (*caça por licença simples*), sport hunting (*caça desportiva*), and commercial hunting (*caça commercial*).[2] The applicable terms and conditions, and the annual hunting quotas for wild animals, as well as the instruments allowed for the practice of

---

[1] Lei No. 10/99, de 7 de Julho, Ministry of Agriculture, art. 6, http://www.minag.gov mz/images/stories/pdf_files/legislacao/LEI%20DE%20FLORESTAS%20E%20FAUNA%20BRAVIA.pdf.

[2] *Id.* art. 20(1).

hunting in the manner provided for in article 20(1) of Law No. 10, must be established by appropriate statute.[3]   Articles 21, 22, and 23 define the above-mentioned hunting categories. Article 24 defines the instruments and means of hunting.

A license is required for the exploitation, trade, use, and transportation of forest and wildlife products by land, river, sea, or air, under the terms of Law No. 10 and all other applicable laws, unless otherwise provided by law.[4]

The Council of Ministers is the competent organ to regulate and ensure the control of forests and wildlife for the purpose of monitoring, orienting, and regulating the activities of preservation, use, and management of forest and wildlife resources.[5]

Every citizen, and in particular the local Councils of Resource Management, as well as license holders, must collaborate by exercising the necessary vigilance to protect the forest and wildlife resources, informing the nearest authorities of violations that they have knowledge of.[6]

In performing their duties, inspectors of forests and wildlife must wear properly identified uniforms and have the right to possession and use of firearms and other equipment to be defined by statute.[7]   The monitoring of forests and wildlife must be exercised by the inspectors of forests and wildlife, by sworn inspectors, and by community agents under the terms and conditions defined by statute.[8]   Inspectors of forests and wildlife are required to seize forest and wildlife products and the instruments used in the commission of a violation.[9]   Vehicles and other means used in the illegal transport of forest and wildlife resources are considered instruments for the purposes of article 37(5) of Law No. 10.[10]   Whenever necessary, inspectors of forests and wildlife, sworn inspectors and community agents, may request the assistance of the nearest authority and police reinforcements to guarantee the performance of their duties.[11]

Article 38(1) of Law No. 10 created stationary and mobile surveillance forest and wildlife posts, which must be duly marked, for the purpose of inspecting forestry and wildlife licensing. According to article 38(2), people and vehicles must stop at forest and wildlife checkpoints whenever requested by inspectors of forests and wildlife, sworn inspectors, or community agents.

---

[3] *Id.* art. 20(2).

[4] *Id.* art. 34.

[5] *Id.* art. 37(1).

[6] *Id.* art. 37(2).

[7] *Id.* art. 37(3).

[8] *Id.* art. 37(4).

[9] *Id.* art. 37(5).

[10] *Id.* art. 37(6).

[11] *Id.* art. 37(7).

Violations of Law No. 10 are punishable with a fine and mandatory measures to restore or compensate the damage caused, without prejudice to other applicable sanctions.[12] The Council of Ministers is responsible for regularly updating of the amounts of the fines provided for in Law No. 10.[13] If the fine is not paid voluntarily, the offender is subject to the consequences provided for in the criminal law in the jurisdiction where the offense was committed, regardless of the appropriate administrative and civil procedures.[14]

The following violations are punishable by a fine of 2,000,000MT[15] (approximately US$69.45) to 100,000,000MT (approximately US$3,472.27):

(a) carrying out any acts of logging without authorization or in breach of the conditions of exploitation;

(b) practicing any acts that disturb or harm the wildlife in protected areas;

(c) hunting without a license or in breach of the conditions established by law;

(d) importing and exporting forest and wildlife resources without a license, or in breach of the conditions established by law;

(e) abandoning forest and wildlife products that are the object of a license.[16]

The following violations are punishable by a fine of 1,000,000MT (approximately US$34.72) to 20,000,000MT (approximately US$694.45):

(a) the storage, transportation, or trade of forest and wildlife resources without authorization or in breach of the conditions established by law;

(b) the receipt of forest and wildlife resources without proper documentation proving that the seller or carrier has the required authorization.[17]

If the violation is committed against rare or endangered species of flora and fauna, as well as any other whose exploitation is prohibited, the fine applicable is ten times the maximum amount specified in article 41 of Law No. 10, without prejudice to other applicable sanctions.[18]

---

[12] *Id.* art. 39(1).

[13] *Id.* art. 39(2).

[14] *Id.* art. 39(3).

[15] Law No. 7 of December 20, 2005, adjusted the Mozambican currency (Metical – MT) by establishing a conversion rate of 1,000, which entered into force on January 1, 2006. Lei No. 7/2005, de 20 de Dezembro, BOLETIM DA REPÚBLICA, I Série – Número 50, http://www.bancomoc mz/Files/DAJ/Lei_7_2005_Taxa%20 de%20Conversao%20Metical%20 Nova%20Familia.pdf. For international transactions, the symbol used for the Mozambican Metical is MZN. NOTAS E MOEDAS DO METICAL, BANCO DE MOÇAMBIQUE (2nd ed.), http://www.bancomoc.mz/ Files/CDI/caderno_online.pdf (last visited Dec. 18, 2012).

[16] *Id.* art. 41(1) (all translations by the author).

[17] *Id.* art. 41(2).

[18] *Id.* art. 41(3).

For the purpose of determining fines, the following are considered aggravating circumstances, in addition to others established by general law:

(a) committing the offense in protected zones;

(b) committing the offense in closed season;

(c) committing the offense against rare, threatened, or endangered species of flora and fauna, so designated by law;

(d) commission of the offense by an inspector of forests and wildlife; sworn inspector; community agent; administrative, police, customs, or maritime authority; or equivalent agent;

(e) committing the offense at night, on Sundays, or on public holidays;

(f) using violence or threats, or resisting supervision in any form;

(g) where the offender, or the person jointly liable, is the possessor of a forest and wildlife license;

(h) using prohibited practices and tools;

(i) committing the offense in organized groups.[19]

For the purpose of determining fines, the following are considered mitigating circumstances, in addition to others established by general law:

(a) first-time offenders;

(b) when the offender voluntarily seeks out inspectors of forests and wildlife to report the damage caused;

(c) when the offender does not have knowledge or awareness of the consequences of the act performed, taking into consideration the person's background, educational level, socioeconomic conditions, regional habits, and place of residence.[20]

The following actors are jointly liable for violations:

(a) the beneficiary of the offense;

(b) whoever facilitates or concurs in carrying out the offense;

(c) inspectors of forests and wildlife, sworn inspectors, and community agents who fail to take the measures provided for in Law No. 10 and its regulations, as well as anyone who has a legal obligation to cooperate in the conduct of surveillance and fails to do so.[21]

The application of fines provided for in Law No. 10 give rise to the following additional penalties:

---

[19] *Id.* art. 42(1).

[20] *Id.* art. 42(2).

[21] *Id.* art. 43.

(a)   reversion in favor of the government of the forest and wildlife products and instruments used in the commission of the offense;

(b)   seizure and cancellation of permits issued in the name of the offender;

(c)   partial or total suspension of the activities causing the offense;

(d)   a ban on receiving new permits for one year.[22]

Products, objects, and instruments seized and declared forfeited to the state under Law No. 10 must be disposed of by one of the following methods:

(a)   sale by auction, except as provided in Law No. 10;

(b)   donation of perishable products to social institutions and nonprofit organizations, after describing them in detail on the apprehension document;

(c)   return of live specimens of flora and wildlife to their area of origin or to the nearest protected area;

(d)   return of instruments belonging to first-time offenders, provided that they are not prohibited, after the payment of fines and compliance with other sanctions or legal obligations.[23]

B. Decree No. 12 of June 6, 2002

Decree No. 12 of June 6, 2002, applies to the activities of protection, preservation, use, exploitation, and production of forest and wildlife resources, which encompasses the trade, transportation, storage, and processing of these resources.[24]

All wildlife that inhabits or travels through the national territory, with the exception of those protected by law, may be hunted.[25] The animals listed in Annex II, which is an integral part of Decree No. 12, are considered protected.[26] Article 44 further prohibits hunting nonadult animals, pregnant females or females accompanied by cubs, or any other animals that may be declared protected by law or convention.[27] Article 46 determines, inter alia, the time and place of hunting and the places where hunting is prohibited, and states that hunting is prohibited during the closed season. Article 47 defines the instruments and means that are allowed to be used for hunting, and article 48 defines the types of firearms that are allowed to be used for hunting. Article 55 determines that hunting is only permitted by those who have a hunting license and all

---

[22] *Id.* art. 44.

[23] *Id.* art. 45.

[24] Decreto No. 12/2002, de 6 de Junho, Ministry of Agriculture, art. 1, http://www.minag.gov.mz/images/stories/pdf_files/legislacao/Regulamento%20da%20Lei%20de%20Florestas%20e%20Fauna%20Bravia.pdf.

[25] *Id.* art. 43(1).

[26] *Id.* art. 43(5).

[27] *Id.* art. 44(b-d).

other documents required by law, and defines the types of hunting licenses and the requirements for obtaining a license.

The Ministry of Agriculture and Rural Development is responsible for the administration, management, and monitoring of activities involving the use of forest and wildlife resources and their existing ecosystems in the national territory,[28] as well as the supervision, monitoring, discipline and orientation of activities for the protection, preservation, use, exploitation and management of forest and wildlife resources.[29]

C. Penal Code

According to article 254 of the Mozambican Penal Code, a person who hunts during the months when hunting is prohibited, or in the months when hunting is permitted but by using prohibited means, is punishable with three days in prison and a fine.[30] The same punishment applies to a person who hunts on land without the consent of the owner; however, the owner must complain about the activity for the punishment to be applicable.[31] The Code is silent with regard to the trafficking of wildlife.

Prepared by Eduardo Soares
Senior Foreign Law Specialist
December 2012

---

[28] *Id.* art. 86.

[29] *Id.* art. 107(1).

[30] CÓDIGO PENAL, Portal do Governo de Moçambique, art, 254, http://www.portaldogoverno.gov mz/Legisla/legisSectores/judiciaria/codigo_penal.pdf (Last Version August 31, 2006).

[31] *Id.* art. 254(sole para.).

LAW LIBRARY OF CONGRESS

SOUTH AFRICA

WILDLIFE TRAFFICKING AND POACHING

Executive Summary

Pursuant to the South African Constitution, legislative jurisdiction regarding the conservation and management of wildlife in South Africa is a concurrent function of the national and provincial governments.

The applicable national legislation, the National Environmental Management: Biodiversity Act (NEMBA) prohibits certain activities defined as "restricted activities," including hunting, selling, transferring, importing, or exporting any threatened or protected animals without a permit. In addition, it imposes further restrictions with regard to particularly vulnerable animals, including absolute bans on hunting and certain hunting methods.

Enforcement of the NEMBA and its subsidiary legislation is primarily the function of the Environmental Management Inspectorate, an organization made up of a network of national, provincial, and municipal government officials. The inspectorate enjoys wide-ranging authority, including inspection, search and seizure, and arrest powers. The South African Police Service (SAPS) also performs some key enforcement functions.

I. Introduction

In South Africa, legislative jurisdiction regarding the conservation and management of wildlife is shared between the national and provincial governments. The Constitution mandates that "[n]ature conservation, excluding national parks, national botanical gardens and marine resources," is one of the functional areas in which there is concurrent national and provincial legislative jurisdiction.[1] South Africa has nine provinces: Eastern Cape, Free State, Gauteng, the KwaZulu-Natal, Limpopo, Mpumalanga, Northern Cape, North West, and Western Cape.[2] A great deal of legislative and executive jurisdiction over issues of conservation and management

---

[1] S. AFR. CONST., 1996, sched. 4, http://www.info.gov.za/documents/constitution/1996/96conssec4 htm.

[2] *South Africa's Provinces*, SOUTH AFRICA GOVERNMENT INFORMATION, http://www.info.gov.za/aboutsa /provinces htm (last visited Jan. 17, 2013).

of wildlife in the country, including regulation of imports and exports, is exercised by these provincial governments.[3]

However, the national government also wields significant legislative jurisdiction over the protection of wildlife, in large part to create national uniformity on the matter. The National Environmental Management: Biodiversity Act (NEMBA) of 2004 and its subsidiary legislation put in place protections for various species that are threatened or otherwise in need of protection.[4] It also provides the authority for consolidating fragmented biodiversity legislation in the country through the establishment of national norms and standards specific to certain particularly vulnerable animals.[5] One example is the National Norms and Standards for the Management of Elephants in South Africa (NNSMESA).[6] One purpose of this document is to set uniform norms and standards so that "the management of elephants is regulated in a way that is uniform across the Republic" and takes into account the country's international obligations.[7]

Enforcement of the NEMBA and its subsidiary legislation is shared across various tiers of government. Specifically, it comes within the jurisdiction of the Environmental Management Inspectorate, a network of national, provincial, and municipal government officials.[8] The Inspectorate enjoys broad enforcement powers, including inspection, search and seizure, and arrest powers, as well as administrative authority to issue compliance notices.[9]

This report focuses on the national laws, specifically the NEMBA and its subsidiary legislation, the application of which is limited to wildlife that is threatened or in need of protection.

---

[3] *Services by Provincial Authorities*, REPUBLIC OF SOUTH AFRICA, DEPARTMENT OF ENVIRONMENTAL AFFAIRS, http://www.environment.gov.za/?q=content/services/provincial-authorities (last visited Jan. 17, 2013); M.A. Kidd, *Environmental Conservation*, *in* 9 THE LAWS OF SOUTH AFRICA 139, 246–47 (LexisNexis Butterworths, 2005).

[4] National Environmental Management: Biodiversity Act No. 10 of 2004 (NEMBA), 20 BUTTERWORTHS STATUTES OF THE REPUBLIC OF SOUTH AFRICA [BSRSA] (rev. through 2011), http://www.info.gov.za/view/DownloadFileAction?id=82170.

[5] *National Environmental Management Act (NEMBA) Regulations on Threatened and Protected Species*, REPUBLIC OF SOUTH AFRICA, DEPARTMENT OF ENVIRONMENTAL AFFAIRS, http://www.speciesstatus.sanbi.org/threatened.aspx (last visited Jan. 23, 2013).

[6] NEMBA: National Norms and Standards for the Management of Elephants in South Africa (NNSMESA), Government Notice [GN] No. 251, GOVERNMENT GAZETTE No. 30833 (Feb. 29, 2008), *available at* the Department of Environment and Tourism website, http://www.environment.gov.za/sites/default/files/gazetted_notices/nemba_elephantsinsa_g30833gon251.pdf.

[7] *Id.* § 2.

[8] National Environmental Management Act 107 of 1998, §§ 1, 31B & 31C, 20 BSRSA (rev. through 2011), *available at* the City of Cape Town's website, http://www.capetown.gov.za/en/EnvironmentalResourceManagement/publications/Documents/NEMA-Act-107-of-1998-incl-all-amendments-effected-until-18Sep2009.pdf; *see also* Department of Environmental Affairs and Tourism, Republic of South Africa, Directorate Enforcement, *Everything You Need to Know About The Environmental Management Inspectorate*, http://www.inece.org/africa/prosecutors/d1_s2b.pdf (last visited Jan. 23, 2012).

[9] National Environmental Management Act 107 of 1998 §§ 31K, 31J, 31L & 31H.

II. Poaching and Trafficking in Wildlife

The NEMBA prohibits anyone from carrying out a "restricted activity" involving any "threatened or protected species" without a permit.[10]   It authorized the Minister of Environmental Affairs and Tourism to establish lists of species that are threatened or in need of national protection, further subdividing the class of "threatened" species into those which are "critically endangered," "endangered," and "vulnerable."[11]   The Minister issued NEMBA Regulations in 2007 that contained such lists.[12]

Restricted activities with regard to the listed species include

(i)   hunting,[13] catching, capturing or killing any living specimen of a listed threatened or protected species by any means, method or device whatsoever, including searching, pursuing, driving, lying in wait, luring, alluring, discharging a missile or injuring with intent to hunt, catch, capture or kill any such specimen;

. . .

(iv)   importing into the Republic, including introducing from the sea, any specimen of a listed threatened or protected species;

(v)   exporting from the Republic, including re-exporting from the Republic, any specimen of a listed threatened or protected species;

(vi)   having in possession or exercising physical control over any specimen of a listed threatened or protected species;

(vii)   growing, breeding or in any other way propagating any specimen of a listed threatened or protected species, or causing it to multiply;

(viii) conveying, moving or otherwise translocating any specimen of a listed threatened or protected species;

---

[10] NEMBA § 57.

[11] NEMBA § 56(1); *see also* DEPARTMENT OF ENVIRONMENTAL AFFAIRS, *supra* note 5.

[12] NEMBA: Publication of Lists of Critically Endangered, Endangered, Vulnerable and Protected Species, No. R. 151, GOVERNMENT GAZETTE No. 29657 (Feb. 23, 2007), *available at* the South African Department of Environmental Affairs and Tourism website, http://www.environment.gov.za/sites/default/files/gazetted notices/nemba_criticallyendangered_protectedspecies_g29657rg8638gon151.pdf. This list was amended by NEMBA: Amendment of Critically Endangered, Endangered, Vulnerable and Protected Species List, GN No. R. 1187, GOVERNMENT GAZETTE No. 30568 (Dec. 14, 2007), http://www.environment.gov.za/sites/default/files/gaz etted_notices/nemba_criticallyendangered_specieslis_g30568rg8801gon1187.pdf.

[13] "Hunting" is assigned a broad definition including "to intentionally kill such species by any means, method or device whatsoever; to capture such species by any means, method or device whatsoever with the intent to kill; to search for, lie in wait for, pursue, shoot at, tranquillise or immobilise such species with the intent to kill; or to lure by any means, method or device whatsoever, such species with the intent to kill, but excludes the culling of a listed threatened or protected species in a protected area or on a registered game farm or the culling of a listed threatened or protected species that has escaped from a protected area and has become a damage causing animal." NEMBA: Threatened or Protected Species Regulations (NEMBA Regulations) § 1, No. R. 152, GOVERNMENT GAZETTE No. 29657 (Feb. 23, 2007), *available at* the South African Department of Environmental Affairs and Tourism website http://www.environment.gov.za/sites/default/files/legislations/nemba_threatenedspecies_regul ations_g29657rg8638gon152.pdf.

(ix)   selling or otherwise trading in, buying, receiving, giving, donating or accepting as a gift, or in any way acquiring or disposing of any specimen of a listed threatened or protected species; or

(x)   any other prescribed activity which involves a specimen of a listed threatened or protected species. [14]

A person who violates these prohibitions, including by violating the terms and conditions stipulated in a permit, commits an offense.[15]

The NEMBA further authorizes the Minister to prohibit any activity "that may negatively impact the survival of listed threatened or protected species," or engaging in such activity without a permit.[16]   These matters are addressed in the 2007 NEMBA Regulations.[17]   A violation of any prohibition issued by the Minister under this authority is an offense under the NEMBA.[18]

The NEMBA Regulations prohibit certain activities involving listed large predators (including cheetah, spotted hyena, brown hyena, wild dog, lion, and leopard), white rhinoceros, and black rhinoceros. It prohibits hunting

---

[14] NEMBA § 1. This does not apply to species in South Africa that are in transit. *Id.* § 57.

[15] *Id.* § 101.

[16] *Id.* § 57.

[17] NEMBA Regulations, *supra* note 13. The Regulations have been amended at least five times through the following measures:

- Threatened or Protected Species Amendment Regulations, GN No. R. 69, GOVERNMENT GAZETTE No. 30703 (Jan. 28, 2008), http://www.environment.gov.za/sites/default/files/legislations/nemba_speciesamendment_g30703rg8825gon69.pdf;

- Threatened or Protected Species Amendment Regulations, 2009, GN No. R. 209, GOVERNMENT GAZETTE No. 31962 (Feb. 27, 2009), http://www.environment.gov.za/sites/default/files/legislations/nemba_species_g31962rg9040gon209.pdf;

- Threatened or Protected Species Second Amendment Regulations, 2009, GN No. R. 210, GOVERNMENT GAZETTE No. 31963 (Feb. 27, 2009), http://www.environment.gov.za/sites/default/files/legislations/nemba_species_g31963rg9041gon210.pdf;

- Threatened or Protected Species Second Amendment Regulations, 2011, GN No. R. 576, GOVERNMENT GAZETTE No. 34453 (July 11, 2011), http://www.environment.gov.za/sites/default/files/legislations/nema_tops_g34453gon576.pdf; and

- Amendment to the Protected Species Regulations, 2007, GN No. R. 614, GOVERNMENT GAZETTE No. 35565 (Aug. 2, 2012), http://www.environment.gov.za/sites/default/files/legislations/nemba_tops_protectedareas_g35565gon614.pdf.

[18] NEMBA § 101.

- a "put and take animal";[19]
- in a controlled environment;
- with the use of any tranquilizer, narcotic, or other immobilizing agent;
- in an area near a holiday facility for such animals;
- with the use of a gin trap; or
- where the hunter does not first obtain a written affidavit from the owner of the land where the animal is located indicating the length of time the animal has been on the property and that it is not a "put and take animal."[20]

The NEMBA Regulations also prohibit the purchase, acquisition, sale, supply, or export of any live animal that is listed as threatened or protected,[21] with one exception: a person may purchase, acquire, sell, supply, or export any of these animals if he can provide an affidavit or other written proof indicating the purpose of the transaction and that the animal is not going to be used for prohibited hunting activities.[22]

The NEMBA Regulations further impose a ban on the use of certain hunting methods by prohibiting the issuance of a permit to hunt a threatened or protected species using

- poison;
- traps;
- snares;
- dogs;
- darts;
- an automatic weapon;
- a weapon discharging a rim firing cartridge of -22 of an inch or smaller caliber; shotguns, except for the hunting of birds; or
- air guns.[23]

The Regulations also prohibit luring such animals for the purpose of hunting using bait, sounds, smell, or any other methods;[24] the use of floodlights or spotlights, motorized vehicles, or

---

[19] A "put and take animal" is defined as "a live specimen of a captive bred listed large predator, or a live specimen of *Cerutotherium simum* (white rhinoceros) or *Diceros bicornis* (black rhinoceros) that is released on a property irrespective of the size of the property for the purpose of hunting the animal within a period of twenty four months." NEMBA Regulations § 1.

[20] *Id.* §§ 1 & 24. These prohibitions are inapplicable to an animal bred and kept in captivity, "which has rehabilitated in an extensive wildlife system and has been fending for itself in an extensive wildlife system for at least twenty-four months." *Id.*

[21] *Id.* § 24.

[22] *Id.*

[23] *Id.*

[24] *Id.*

aircraft;[25] and hunting an animal not in control of all its faculties due to a tranquilizing, narcotic, or other immobilizing agent, or cornered with no chance to escape.[26]

The violation of any of the above-referenced provisions of the NEMBA Regulations is an offense.[27] Limited exceptions apply to the Regulations' prohibitions, however.

In addition to the above-referenced prohibitions under the NEMBA and the NEMBA Regulations, national norms and standards issued under the NEMBA impose further restrictions regarding specific animals—for example, the National Norms and Standards for the Management of Elephants in South Africa (NNSMESA). The NNSMESA prohibits elephant hunting except for the hunting of solitary males, female elephants that cause damages provided all applicable procedures are followed, and female elephants on private or communal land according to a management plan, and imposes specific restrictions applicable to the hunting of these elephants.[28] When the elephant hunter is an alien, a registered professional hunter must be present for each hunt.[29]

The NNSMESA also imposes additional restrictions on hunting methods in addition to those provided under the NEMBA and the NEMBA Regulations. It specifically prohibits the following methods:

(a) driving an elephant by any means;
(b) hunting within 500 metres of a water hole or watering point;
(c) using a pitfall; or
(d) hunting with –
    (i) a rifle with a calibre of less than .375 H&H; and
    (ii) a bullet with a full metal jacket or monolithic construction with a weight of not less than 286 grains or heavier bullet of monolithic or full metal jacket construction.[30]

In addition the NNSMESA imposes various restrictions on the translocation, import, and export of elephants.[31]

Violation of any of the NNSMESA provisions (including by a person who owns or possesses land in which an elephant roams or a person who is a management authority of a protected area) is an offense under the NEMBA Regulations.[32]

---

[25] *Id.*

[26] *Id.*

[27] *Id.* § 73. *See* discussion of corresponding penalties, Part III(B), *infra.*

[28] National Norms and Standards for the Management of Elephants in South Africa § 20.

[29] *Id.*

[30] *Id.* § 21.

[31] *Id.* § 12.

[32] NEMBA Regulations § 73.

Additional norms and standards issued under the NEMBA focus on hunting methods.[33] These establish national standards on

    (a) minimum bullet weights for rifle hunting;
    (b) minimum bullet weights and barrel lengths for handgun hunting;
    (c) permissible bows for bow hunting;
    (d) minimum requirements for bow hunting;

    (e) minimum requirements for falconry;
    (f) criteria to be met by game birds for inclusion in provincial hunting proclamations.[34]

Also issued under the authority established by the NEMBA are the Norms and Standards dealing with rhinoceros hunting and tracking,[35] which establish national standards for "the marking of rhinoceros and rhinoceros horn and for the hunting of rhinoceros for trophy hunting purposes."[36]

III. Penalties

A. Under NEMBA

A person convicted of an offense under the above-referenced provisions of the NEMBA is subject to fines and/or up to five years of imprisonment.[37] If the conviction is for an offense regarding a listed threatened or protected animal, the applicable fine could reach up to three times the value of the animal.[38]

B. Under NEMBA Regulations

A person convicted under any of the above-referenced provisions of the NEMBA Regulations is subject to a fine in the amount of 100,000 South African Rand (ZAR) (about US$11,255) and/or up to five years of imprisonment.[39]

---

[33] NEMBA: Norms and Standards for Hunting Methods in South Africa, GN No. 456, GOVERNMENT GAZETTE No. 34326 (May 27, 2011), http://faolex fao.org /docs/pdf/saf104522.pdf.

[34] *Id.* § 2.

[35] NEMBA: The Norms and Standards for the Marking of Rhinoceros and Rhinoceros Horn, and for the Hunting of Rhinoceros for Trophy Hunting Purposes, GN No. 304, GOVERNMENT GAZETTE No. 35248 (Apr. 10, 2012), http://www.environment.gov.za/sites/default/files/gazetted_notices/nemba_huntingstandards_g35248gen304.pdf.

[36] *Id.*

[37] NEMBA § 102.

[38] *Id.*

[39] NEMBA Regulations § 74.

C. Penalties of General Application

In addition to the penalties for an offense under the NEMBA or its subsidiary legislation, two generally applicable additional penalties may apply: a court may order that the offender's permit or authorization, if any, be revoked or that the offender be disqualified from being eligible for one,[40] or order that any tool used in the commission of the crime be forfeited to the state.[41]

IV. Enforcement Authority

The Environmental Management Inspectorate—an institution consisting of a network of enforcement officials known as Enforcement Management Inspectors (EMIs) who represent national, provincial, and municipal authorities—is the principal enforcement authority for the NEMBA and its subsidiary legislation.[42] EMIs enjoy broad administrative and enforcement powers, including the power to

- conduct routine warrantless inspections of buildings, land, vehicles, vessels, aircrafts, containers, bags, etc. to ensure compliance with the controlling law or terms of a permit;[43]

- conduct warrantless searches and seize vehicles, vessels, aircraft, or pack animals on the basis of any "reasonable suspicion" that they are being used in the commission of a crime or in violation of the controlling law or the terms of a permit, or contain evidence of an offense or a violation;[44]

- issue a compliance notice upon discovering that a person has failed to comply with the terms of the controlling law or a permit issued under the law;[45] and

- make arrests.[46]

The Environmental Management Inspectorate does not have prosecutorial powers.[47]

In addition, members of the South African Police Service (SAPS) also enjoy all the enforcement powers conferred on the EMIs with two notable exceptions: the power to conduct routine searches and the power to issue compliance notices.[48]

---

[40] National Environmental Management Act 107 of 1998, § 34C.

[41] *Id.* § 34D.

[42] *Id.* §§ 1, 31B & 31C; *see also* Department of Environmental Affairs and Tourism, *supra* note 8, at 1.

[43] The National Environmental Management Act 107 of 1998, § 31K. Routine inspection of residential premises requires a warrant or consent of the resident. *Id.*

[44] *Id.* § 31J.

[45] *Id.* § 31L.

[46] *Id.* § 31H.

[47] Department of Environmental Affairs and Tourism, *supra* note 8, at 5.

[48] The National Environmental Management Act 107 of 1998, § 31O.

Prepared by Hanibal Goitom
Foreign Law Specialist
January 2013

2013–008667

LAW LIBRARY OF CONGRESS

TANZANIA

WILDLIFE TRAFFICKING AND POACHING

Executive Summary

Tanzania has a highly fragmented national wildlife management and conservation regulatory regime in which three different laws control poaching: the Wildlife Conservation Act (WCA), the National Parks Act (NPA), and the Forest Resources Management and Conservation Act (FRMCA). All three criminalize poaching and prescribe an assortment of penalties for poaching-related offenses, which are by and large tied to the types of animals involved in the offending.

With regard to the issue of trafficking, the WCA appears to be the sole controlling legislation.

The enforcement mechanisms for these laws are divided across several organizations that cover specific areas of the country. These include the Wildlife Authority, the Forest Authority (Zanzibar), and the Board of Trustees of the Tanzania National Parks. While all three have sweeping search, seizure, and arrest authority, only the latter two enjoy prosecutorial powers.

I. Introduction

Wildlife is crucial to Tanzania's economy, as it sustains millions of the country's rural population.[1] It is also the keystone to the tourism industry—a sector that accounts for about 17% of the country's gross domestic product (GDP) and is the largest source of foreign exchange.[2] The contribution of the country's wildlife to the economy is largely through "hunting concessions, trophy licenses, export of live animals, and from non-consumptive tourism."[3]

---

[1] Fred Nelson et al., *The Evolution and Reform of Tanzania Wildlife Management*, 5(2) CONSERVATION AND SOCIETY 232, 233–34 (2007), http://www.conservationandsociety.org/article.asp?issn=0972-4923;year=2007;volume=5;issue=2;spage=232;epage=261;aulast=Nelson.

[2] *Id.*; WORLD RESOURCE INSTITUTE, FOCUS OF LAND IN AFRICA BRIEF: TANZANIA 2 (Aug. 2010), http://www.wri.org/property-rights-africa/wriTest_Tanzania//documents/Tanzania_LessonBrief_4.pdf.

[3] J.R. Kideghesho, Who Pays for Wildlife Conservation in Tanzania and Who Benefits? (Conference Paper, 2008), *available at* http://dlc.dlib.indiana.edu/dlc/ bitstream/handle/10535/587/Kideghesho_102301.pdf?sequence=1.

Tanzania's wildlife management system reflects this fact.   The country has sixteen national parks that cover an area of over forty-two thousand square kilometers.[4]   It has the "largest protected area estate in Africa, both absolutely and relatively."[5]   About 40% of the country is designated as protected estate.[6]

However, the wildlife management system is not without problems.   For instance, the process of allocating and monitoring hunting concessions is said to be riddled with widespread corruption.[7]   The Minister of Natural Resources and Tourism and top Wildlife Department officials were recently fired for taking bribes in exchange for assigning hunting blocks and allowing over a hundred live animals to be shipped abroad.[8]   Poaching is another, grave problem.[9]   Difficulties in collecting evidence and flaws in the criminal justice system make it challenging to prosecute offenders.[10]

While various laws govern wildlife conservation,[11] only a few are relevant to the issues of wildlife poaching and trafficking.   The Wildlife Conservation Act (WCA)[12] and the National Parks Act (NPA)[13] as well as their subsidiary legislation are the controlling laws in mainland

---

[4] WORLD RESOURCE INSTITUTE, *supra* note 2, at 2.

[5] Dan Brockington et al., *Preserving the New Tanzania: Conservation and Land Use Change*, 41(3) INT'L. J. AFR. HIST. STUD. 557, 557 (2008).

[6] Peter G. Veit & Catherine Benson, *When Parks and People Collide, Human Rights Dialogue: "Environmental Rights"*, CARNEGIE COUNCIL FOR ETHICS IN INTERNATIONAL AFFAIRS (Apr. 23, 2004), http://www.carnegiecouncil.org/publications/archive/dialogue/2_11/section_2/4449.html.

[7] Tor A. Benjaminsen et al., Wildlife Management in Tanzania: Recentralization, Rent Seeking, and Resistance 16–17 (Conference Paper, International Institute of Social Studies in The Hague, 2011), http://www.iss. nl/fileadmin/ASSETS/iss/Documents/Conference_presentations/NatureInc_Tor_A._Benjaminsen.pdf.

[8] John Burnett, *Poachers Decimate Tanzania's Elephant*, NPR (Oct. 25, 2012), http://www.npr.org/ 2012/10/25/163563426/poachers-decimate-tanzanias-elephant-herds.

[9] John Burnett, *In a Tanzanian Village, Elephant Poachers Thrive*, NPR (Oct. 25, 2012), http://www.npr.org/2012/10/25/163629043/in-a-tanzanian-village-elephant-poachers-thrive.

[10] *New Tool in Fight Against Bushmeat Poaching in Tanzania*, WILDLIFE EXTRA (Dec. 2012), http://www.wildlifeextra.com/go/news/serengeti-bushmeat.html#cr.

[11] These include: the Forest Act of 2002; the National Parks Ordinance of 1959; the Fisheries Act of 1970, the Marine Parks and Reserves Act of 1994; the Ngorongoro Conservation Ordinance; and the Wildlife Conservation Act of 1974 (now repealed by the Wildlife Conservation Act of 2009).   Patricia Kameri-Mboote, *Sustainable Management of Wildlife Resources in East Africa: A Critical Analysis of the Legal, Policy and Institutional Frameworks* 5 (Int'l Environmental Law Research Centre, Working Paper No. 2005-5, 2005), http://www.ielrc.org/content/w0505.pdf; KALEB LAMECK GAMAYA, LEGAL AND HUMAN RIGHTS CENTRE, SELECTED ISSUES FOR TANZANIAN LAW REFORM: A REVIEW ANALYSIS AND RECOMMENDATION FOR REFORM 16 (2002).

[12] The Wildlife Conservation Act No. 5 of 2009, *available at* the Tanzanian Parliament website, http://polis.parliament.go.tz/PAMS/docs/5-2009.pdf.   It has not been possible to locate any subsidiary legislation that may be applicable.

[13] The National Parks Act, VII LAWS OF TANZANIA: PRINCIPAL LEGISLATION, Cap. 282 (rev. ed. 2002).

Tanzania. In the semiautonomous region of Zanzibar, the governing law appears to be the Forest Resources Management and Conservation Act (FRMCA).[14]

The task of enforcing the controlling laws is equally fragmented. While the WCA authorizes the establishment of an autonomous body, the Wildlife Authority, to enforce the provisions in mainland Tanzania, the Authority's reach will not extend to the Ngorongoro Conservation Area and the national parks. The task of protecting wildlife resources in the national parks is vested in the Board of Trustees of the Tanzania National Parks, while the Ngorongoro Conservation Area Authority is tasked with the same role in the Ngorongoro Conservation Area. In addition to the planned Wildlife Authority, which when established will be the main enforcement agency, various other government bodies including the police also enjoy some enforcement authority. In Zanzibar, the Forest Authority is the primary enforcer of the FRMCA.

II. The Wildlife Conservation Act

A. Poaching and Trafficking in Wildlife

1. Hunting in Certain Places

Hunting, defined by the WCA as "any act directed or incidental to the killing of any animal," is prohibited in a game reserve, game controlled area, or wetlands reserve without a permit or in violation of the terms of a permit.[15] The penalties vary depending on the animal involved (*see* Table 1.).

Table 1.[16]

Category	List of Animals	Penalty
WCA *First Schedule*, Part I	**Animals** Sanje Mangabey, oryx, leopard, cheetah, black rhinoceros, highland mangabey, klipspringer, wild dog, abbotts duiker, buffalo, rosevelt sable, hyrax, zebra, giant elephant shrew, puku, lion,	Imprisonment from five to ten years and/or a fine ranging from 500,000 Tanzanian Shilling (TZS) (about US$315) to 2 million TZS (about US$1260).

---

[14] Forest Resources Management and Conservation Act No. 10 of 1996, Cv BILL SUPPLEMENT TO THE REVOLUTIONARY GOVERNMENT OF ZANZIBAR GAZETTE (Oct. 19, 1996) (note that it was not possible to locate the finalized version of the Act or any subsidiary legislation that may be applicable); *see also* Martin Walsh & Kelle Goldman, *Chasing Imaginary Leopards: Science, Witchcraft and the Politics of Conservation in Zanzibar*, 6(4) J. EAST AFR. STUD. 727, 732 (Nov. 2012), *available at* Taylor & Francis Online, http://www.tandfonline .com/doi/pdf/10.1080/17531055.2012.729778.

[15] Wildlife Conservation Act § 19.

[16] *Id.*

Category	List of Animals	Penalty
	caracal, roberts gazelle, gerenuk, lesser kudu, African elephant, mountain-reedbuck **Birds** ShoebilJ (whale headed stock), wattled crane, peregrin falcon, udzungwa forest partridge, green pigeon **Reptiles** Slender Snorted Crocodile **Amphibians** Kihansi Spray Toad **National Game** National Game	
WCA *First Schedule*, Part II	African clawless otter, spotted necked otter, hippopotamus, roan antelope, waterbuck-common, waterbuck-defassa, nile crocodile, ostrich, topi, sable antelope, eland, greater kudu.	Imprisonment from two to five years and/or a fine ranging from 200TZS (about US$13) to 500TZS (about US$31).
WCA *First Schedule*, Part III	All other animals	Imprisonment from one to three years' and/or a fine ranging from 100,000TZS (about US$69) to 1 million TZS (about US$630).

All other offenses are punishable by a fine ranging from 200,000TZS (about US$126) to 500,000TZS or one to six months' imprisonment.[17]

The WCA prohibits the hunting of any protected species[18] in "species management areas."[19] The penalties vary depending on the animal. If the offense involves a protected

---

[17] *Id.*

species, harsh penalties are imposed—imprisonment of three to seven years and/or a fine in the amount of at least twice the value of the animal involved.[20] All other offenses are punishable by a prison term ranging from three months to two years or a fine ranging from 100,000TZS to 500,000TZS.[21]

Hunting national game (any animal or class of animals declared as such by the Minister of Natural Resources and Tourism) without first obtaining a permit is also an offense. Illegal hunting in this regard is punishable by a prison term ranging from one to five years or a fine equivalent to at least twice the value of the animal.[22] All other offenses, including a violation of the terms of a permit, are punishable by imprisonment of one to three years or a fine ranging from 300,000TZS (about US$189) to 1 million TZS (about US$630).[23]

2. Hunting of Certain Animals

The WCA makes it an offense to hunt a "specified animal"[24] or a "scheduled animal"[25] without a license or in violation of the terms of one.[26] Every license includes information regarding the species approved for hunting, the number of animals that may be hunted by the holder of a license, the place where such animal may be hunted, and an expiration date.[27] The penalties for any violation vary depending on the animal involved (*see* Table 2.):

---

[18] These include species that have been declared protected species by the Minister of Natural Resources and Tourism, and species found in or migrate to or through Tanzania and that are protected under an international treaty to which Tanzania is a state party. *Id.* § 94.

[19] *Id.* § 24. Species management area is "an area subject to active intervention for management purposes in order to ensure the maintenance of habitat or to meet the requirements of specific species." *Id.* § 3.

[20] *Id.* § 24.

[21] *Id.*

[22] *Id.* § 25.

[23] *Id.*

[24] Animals listed in the *Second Schedule* of the WCA including dikdik, eland, bushbuck and impala, pigmy goose, spur fowl, Egyptian goose, and white-backed duck. *Id.* § 3.

[25] Animals listed in the *Third Schedule* of the WCA including golden jackal, python, leopard, wild cat, harlequin quail and common quail. *Id.*

[26] *Id.* § 47.

[27] *Id.* §§ 46 & 47.

Table 2.[28]

Category	List of Animals	Penalty
WCA *First Schedule,* Part I	*See* Table 1.	Imprisonment from three to ten years and possible fine in the amount of at least twice the value of the animal involved.
WCA *First Schedule,* Part II	*See* Table 1.	Imprisonment from two to five years possible fine in the amount of at least twice the value of the animal involved.
WCA *First Schedule,* Part III	*See* Table 1.	Imprisonment from one to three years and possible fine in the amount of at least twice the value of the animal involved.

Specifying the limit on the number of animals that may be hunted on a license may not be an effective safeguard against unlimited hunting of specified or scheduled animals. A recent news article on poaching in South Africa, where a similar limit is said to be in place, discussed how international crime syndicates routinely sidestep such limits by simply convincing more people to obtain licenses.[29] This creates a serious problem, especially if there is no general ceiling on the number of licenses that may be issued within a certain time period. However, the fact that the WCA criminalizes the transfer of a license or a permit issued for one person to another,[30] if effectively policed, may possibly minimize violations. In this situation, the WCA holds both the person to whom the license or permit was legally issued and the person who obtains it by fraud criminally responsible.[31]

3. Hunting Methods

Section 65(1) of the WCA prohibits the use of the following hunting methods without first seeking and obtaining written authorization:

---

[28] *Id.* § 47.

[29] Jeffrey Gettleman, *Coveting Horns, Ruthless Smugglers' Rings Put Rhinos in the Cross Hairs*, THE NEW YORK TIMES (Dec. 31, 2012), http://www.nytimes.com/2013/01/01/world/ africa/ruthless-smuggling-rings-put-rhinos-in-the-cross-hairs.html?hp.

[30] Wildlife Conservation Act § 104.

[31] *Id.* §§ 104 &105

(a) use for the purpose of hunting any animal –
   (i)   any mechanically propelled vehicle;
   (ii)   any poison, bait, poisoned bait, poisoned weapon, stakes, net, gin, trap, set gun, pitfall, missile, explosives, ball ammunition, snare, hide, spear, fence or enclosure;
   (iii) a dog or any domesticated animal;
   (iv)   any automatic or semi automatic firearm capable of firing more than one cartridge as a result of one pressure of the trigger or of reloading itself more than once without further action by the operator;
   (v)   any device capable of reducing or designed to reduce the sound made by the discharge of any firearm;
   (vi)   any artificial light or flare, night vision devises; or
   (vii) any anaesthetic dart capable of immobilisation;

(b) in the process of hunting any animal cause any fire; and

(c) hunt any animal –

   (i)   from any mechanically propelled vehicle or within two hundred metres of such vehicle, except when hunting birds in water;
   (ii)   other than a hippopotamus, otter, sitatunga, puku, crocodile, water-buck or bird within five hundred metres of any permanent water, pool, waterhole or salt-lick;
   (iii) within one kilometre of a national park, a zoo, game sanctuary, the Ngorongoro Conservation Area or an aerodrome; and
   (iv)   during the hours of darkness.[32]

Use of the any of these prohibited methods is an offense punishable by one to three years' imprisonment and/or a fine ranging from 1 to 2 million TZS.[33]   If the offense relates to the hunting or killing of an animal, the WCA imposes a mandatory minimum fine equivalent to an amount twice the value of the animal.[34]

The WCA also prohibits the use of certain methods or tools that may be a danger to animals in game reserves, wetlands reserves, and game controlled areas, stating,

> (1) Any person shall not within any game reserve, wetlands reserve or game controlled area–
>
> (a) dig, lay, or construct any pitfall, net, trap, snare or use other device whatsoever, capable of killing, capturing or wounding any animal; or
> (b) carry or have in his possession or under his control any weapon in respect of which he fails to satisfy the Director that it was intended to be used for a purpose other than hunting, killing, wounding or capturing of an animal[.][35]
> . . .

---

[32] *Id.* § 65. A limited exception may apply with regard to the hunting of a wounded dangerous animal, an animal specified in the *Fourth Schedule* of the WCA. *Id.* §§ 3 & 72. Hours of darkness includes a time period "commencing at 6.30 p.m. on any day and expiring at 5.30 a m. on the following day." *Id.* § 3.

[33] *Id.* § 65(1).

[34] *Id.*

[35] *Id.* § 20.

A violation of these bans is an offense punishable by imprisonment ranging from six months to two years and/or 200,000 to 2 million TZS in fines.[36]

Hunting during the closed season is also prohibited except when a permit is issued. The penalties for a violation of this provision vary depending on the animal involved.[37] If the offense involves an animal listed in Part I of the Wildlife Conservation Act's *First Schedule*, the penalty is three to five years' imprisonment.[38] If it involves an animal listed in Part II of the *First Schedule*, a penalty of two to five years' imprisonment applies.[39] If it involves an animal listed in Part III of the *First Schedule*, the applicable penalty is one to three years' imprisonment.[40] In addition to incarceration, the court has the discretion in all three of these cases to impose a fine in the amount of twice the value of the animal involved.[41] In all other cases the penalty is six to twelve months' imprisonment and/or a 300,000TZS to 2 million TZS fine.[42]

B. Dealing in Trophies

The WCA imposes bans with regard to the selling, buying, transferring, transporting, accepting, exporting, or importing of trophies.[43] It specifically bans

- dealing in a trophy, manufacturing an article from a trophy for sale, or carrying on the business of a trophy dealer without a license;

- accepting, buying, manufacturing an article from, selling, or transferring an unregistered trophy;

- transferring a trophy without a permit;

- exporting or re-exporting any trophy without a trophy export certificate or, when the export involves species listed in the Convention on International Trade in Endangered Species of Wild Fauna and Flora (CITES), export without a CITES permit; and

- importing a trophy without a proper permit and without compliance with the provisions of CITES.[44]

---

[36] *Id.*

[37] *Id.* § 28.

[38] *Id.*

[39] *Id.*

[40] *Id.*

[41] *Id.*

[42] *Id.*

[43] "Trophy" is defined as "any animal alive or dead, and any horn, ivory, tooth, tursh, bone, claw, hoof, skin, meat, hair, feather, egg or other portion of any animal and includes a manufactured trophy." *Id.* § 3.

[44] *Id.* §§ 80-83.

Violation of any of these provisions is an offense punishable by two to five years' imprisonment and/or a fine equivalent to twice the value of the trophy.[45] If the offense involves the import, export, or re-export of a trophy in violation of the above bans or CITES provisions, the trophy is subject to confiscation.[46]

C. Penalties of General Application

In addition to the penalties discussed above, the WCA also imposes further punishment in the form of forfeiture. Accordingly, whenever a person is convicted of any offense under the WCA, the court is in most cases required to order the forfeiture of any tool used in the commission of the crime (including a weapon, any item used for storing or processing an animal; game meat or trophies; and vehicles, tents, or camping equipment) as well as the fruits of the crime.[47]

The WCA imposes an evidentiary standard in which the prosecution is not required to prove the charges against a suspect beyond a reasonable doubt. The evidentiary standard used in various cases, including poaching cases, places the burden on the defendant to prove that the animal in question was killed legally.[48]

D. Enforcement Authority

The WCA authorizes the establishment of a Wildlife Authority, which will be the law's principal enforcer. The Authority, an autonomous body, will be primarily involved in "the protection, management and administration of wildlife resources outside the Ngorongoro Conservation Area and National Parks."[49] The Authority is to include a paramilitary unit, the Wildlife Protection Unit, whose functions will include "protection of wildlife against unlawful utilization relating to hunting, capturing and photographing of wildlife and securing of trophies."[50] The Ministry of Natural Resources and Tourism is said to be in the final stages of establishing this Authority.[51] At the moment, enforcement authority appears to rest with the Wildlife Division of the Ministry.[52]

In addition to the Wildlife Authority, the WCA gives members of several other government institutions some enforcement authority. These include the police and select

---

[45] *Id.* § 84.

[46] *Id.*

[47] *Id.* § 111.

[48] *Id.* § 75.

[49] *Id.* § 8.

[50] *Id.* §§ 10, 11.

[51] *Wildlife Authority to be Established Soon*, DAILY NEWS (ONLINE EDITION) (July 26, 2012), http://www.dailynews.co.tz/index.php/parliament-news/7887-wildlife-authority-to-be-established-soon.

[52] *Wildlife Division*, THE UNITED REPUBLIC OF TANZANIA MINISTRY OF NATURAL RESOURCES AND TOURISM, http:// www.mnrt.go.tz/index.php?option=com_content&view=section&layout=blog&id=10&Itemid=13 (last visited Jan. 11, 2013).

members of various other institutions, including the Forest and Beekeeping Division, the national parks, the Ngorongoro Conservation Area, the Fisheries Division, Wildlife Management Areas, the Marine Parks and Reserve, the Antiquities Division, and any other person so appointed.[53]

The WCA gives all above-listed enforcers, also known as authorized officers, broad search, seizure, and arrest powers. Whenever any authorized officer has "reasonable ground" to believe that an offense has been or is about to be committed, he is authorized to demand that a person produce "any animal, game meat, trophy or weapon" for inspection.[54] Such officer may also conduct warrantless searches of "any land, building, tent, vehicle, aircraft, vessel, or bag" in the possession of such person.[55] In addition, an authorized officer may seize any of the above-listed items in the control of the suspect.[56] Other authorities of an authorized officer include inspecting licensed premises of trophy dealers and arresting anyone who has violated provisions of the law.[57]

III. The National Parks Act

A. Poaching

The NPA prohibits hunting within a national park of any animal or fish, with the exception of "domestic animals," without a permit.[58] The penalty for violation of this ban depends on the animal involved:

Table 3.[59]

Category	List of Animals	Penalty
WCA *First Schedule*, Part I	*See* Table 1.	Imprisonment from three- to five-years and a possible additional penalty of up to 100,000TZS in fines.
WCA *First Schedule*, Part II	*See* Table 1.	Imprisonment from two- to five-years and possible additional fines of up to 50,000TZS.

---

[53] Wildlife Conservation Act § 3.

[54] *Id.* § 106.

[55] *Id.* When entering into a dwelling house to conduct a warrantless search, authorized officers should make sure that there is at least one independent person present. *Id.*

[56] *Id.*

[57] *Id.*

[58] The National Parks Act § 23.

[59] *Id.*

Category	List of Animals	Penalty
WCA *First Schedule*, Part III	*See* Table 1.	Imprisonment from one to three years and possible additional fines of up to 20,000TZS.

All other offenses are punishable by a fine in the range of 3,000 to 20,000TZS or a prison term of three months to three years.[60]

The NPA also bans placing anything that may kill an animal (including a pitfall, net, trap, or snare) or carrying a weapon, the purpose of which is to hunt an animal within a national park.[61] A violation of this provision is an offense punishable by a prison term of up to two years and/or a fine of up to 20,000TZS.[62]

B. Penalties of General Application

If a person commits an offense under the NPA and no specific penalty is applicable, the person is liable to a fine of up to 10,000TZS and/or imprisonment of up to one year.[63] In addition to these penalties, the NPA gives courts the discretion to impose the penalty of forfeiture of any tools used in the commission of a crime.[64]

The NPA contains the same evidentiary standard as the WCA, placing the burden of proof on the defendant.[65]

C. Enforcement Authority

Enforcement of the provisions of the NPA is the primary function of the Trustees of the Tanzania National Parks. The NPA states that the Trustees' functions, among others, include controlling, managing, and maintaining national parks.[66]

The Trustees enjoy wide enforcement powers. They have search, seizure, and arrest powers identical to those of authorized officers under the WCA.[67] In addition, they enjoy

---

[60] *Id.*

[61] *Id.* § 24.

[62] *Id.*

[63] *Id.* § 29.

[64] *Id.*

[65] *Id* § 31.

[66] *Id.* § 17.

[67] *Id.* § 31.

prosecutorial powers and the power to delegate the authority to prosecute in subordinate courts for any and all violations of the NPA provisions and all its subsidiary legislation.[68]

IV. Forest Resources Management and Conservation Act (FRMCA)

A. Poaching

The FRMCA prohibits hunting or fishing in a Forest Reserve (any land in Zanzibar so declared by the Minister responsible for the management and conservation of forest resources) and any other restricted area without a license.[69] It also bans use of certain methods of hunting, including setting a "trap, snare or net" or using or possessing "any gun, poison or explosive substance."[70] Violation of these bans is an offense punishable by at least six months' imprisonment and/or a fine in the amount of at least 50,000TZS.[71]

The FRMCA also requires the Minister to issue regulations extending further protection for certain wild animals that are "endangered or threatened with extinction."[72] Animals on this list can only be hunted with a special permit issued for the purpose of scientific research, conservation, culling, or control; or in defense of a human life.[73] Violation of any such regulations is an offense for which the FRMCA stipulates a minimum prison term of six months and/or a fine in the amount of at least 50,000TZS.[74]

B. Penalties of General Application

The FRMCA provides further penalties in addition to those stated above. If a court convicts a person for violation of any of the law's provisions, it is required to issue an order revoking the person's license, if any,[75] and must also order the person to pay ten times the amount of any royalties and other fees that would have been payable if the act for which the person was convicted had been duly authorized.[76] The court is further required to issue an order to compel the person to reimburse the Forest Authority for any costs incurred in connection with the offense.[77] In addition, recidivism within two years from the commission of the previous offense automatically doubles the amount of fines and/or the prison term stipulated for the offense.[78]

---

[68] *Id.* § 27.

[69] Forest Resources Management and Conservation Act § 33.

[70] *Id.*

[71] *Id.* § 89.

[72] *Id.* § 74. It has not been possible to locate any regulation to this effect.

[73] *Id* § 75.

[74] *Id.* § 92.

[75] *Id.* § 97.

[76] *Id.*

[77] *Id.*

[78] *Id.* § 98.

C. Enforcement Authority

Enforcing the FRMCA is the primary task of the Forest Authority. Among other things, the Forest Authority is required by law to "take appropriate measures to protect and regulate the hunting . . . of wildlife animals."[79] However, the Forest Administrator may expand the enforcement authority by appointing any forest officer to be an enforcement officer.[80]

An enforcement officer has far-reaching inspection, seizure, and arrest powers. He may require any person to produce a license or conduct warrantless searches of any vehicle or building that he reasonably suspects is being used in connection with an act that violates the FRMCA.[81] The enforcement officer also has the authority to seize anything he finds during a search, "which appears to be" used in committing an offense under the law.[82] Significantly, an enforcement officer has the authority to arrest anyone whom he reasonably suspects has committed an offense if the person refuses to cooperate or if the officer has reason to believe he is a flight risk.[83]

In addition, enforcement officers enjoy wide prosecutorial powers and may, at their discretion, prosecute anyone suspected of committing an offense under the FRMCA before a magistrate.[84]

Prepared by Hanibal Goitom
Foreign Law Specialist
January 2013

---

[79] *Id.* § 6.

[80] *Id.* § 9.

[81] *Id.* § 84.

[82] *Id.* § 85.

[83] *Id.* § 87.

[84] *Id.* § 88.